VEGAN SLOW COOKING

FOR TWO —OR— JUST FOR YOU

More Than 100
Delicious One-Pot Meals for Your 1.5-Quart or 1.5-Litre Slow Cooker

KATHY HESTER
best-selling author of *The Vegan Slow Cooker*

FAIR WINDS
PRESS
BEVERLY, MASSACHUSETTS

First published in the USA in 2013 by
Fair Winds Press, a member of
Quayside Publishing Group
100 Cummings Center
Suite 406-L
Beverly, MA 01915-6101
www.fairwindspress.com
Visit www.QuarrySPOON.com and help us celebrate food and culture one spoonful
at a time!

17 16 15 14 13   1 2 3 4 5

ISBN: 978-1-59233-563-3

Digital edition published in 2013
eISBN: 978-1-61058-926-0

Library of Congress Cataloging-in-Publication Data available

Cover and Book design by Duckie Designs
Photography by: Kate Lewis www.kk-Lewis.com
Food and Prop Styling by: Kate Lewis
Food Styling by: Heidi Robb on selected photography
Photography Assistance by: Maryellen Echle

Printed and bound in China

*The information in this book is for educational purposes only. It is not intended to
replace the advice of a physician or medical practitioner. Please see your health care
provider before beginning any new health program.*

This book is dedicated to my family and friends for putting up with me while I wrote two books in one year and for being so patient and supportive. I promise you many cocktail parties and fancy dinners at my house in the very near future!

—CONTENTS—

CHAPTER ONE

THE LITTLE SLOW COOKER THAT CAN!

IF YOU'RE NEW TO COOKING VEGAN OR USING A SLOW COOKER, let me be the first to congratulate you on trying something new! Cooking for a small family, or just yourself, has its benefits. All your groceries will actually fit into your fridge, and you won't end up needing a full-sized freezer just to store the leftovers from a giant slow cooker.

The little slow cooker, 1½ to 2 quarts (1.5 to 2 L) in size, is so easy to use that it makes cooking every day a snap, so you can enjoy a variety of healthy foods at a fraction of the cost of eating out. Having a different meal every night is much better than making a big pot of chili and eating it for seven days straight.

Stay open-minded and you'll find a whole new world of food to fall in love with. There's Thai Massaman Curry (page 109), Indian-Stuffed Eggplant and Tempeh Tandoori (page 144), and even an All-in-One Thanksgiving Dinner (page 141) you can have any day of the year. You'll be amazed at what you can do with your little slow cooker!

Over the years I've cooked for myself, my partner, and my friends when they had their first child. All of these situations involve families of one kind or another for which you can easily create healthy meals with your slow cooker. And with just a little effort, you, too, will be cooking delicious meals that your small family will love. Inside, you'll find some great tips and tricks on using your slow cooker along with a few hints to save both time and effort. My small slow cooker recipes are some of my most popular ones on my blog, healthyslowcooking.com. It can be difficult to face the task of making dinner from scratch when you've been working all day. But with a little planning, you can walk in and sit down right away to eat your dinner every night.

SMALL SLOW COOKER TIPS AND TRICKS

If you're new to the small 1½- to 2-quart (1.5 to 2 L) slow cooker, your world is about to change for the better. On my blog, I often talk about people getting one, two, or even three of them. You really don't want to know just how many I've accumulated while writing this book!

For testing the recipes for this book, I, along with my amazing testers, used modern 1½- or 2-quart (1.5 to 2 L) slow cookers. If you have an older one, say a Crockette, you will need to adjust the liquids down, as older models don't run as hot and therefore don't burn off as much liquid. Many modern ones run much hotter. Some will boil and others won't, but once you get used to your slow cooker, you'll know how to adjust any recipes in it. Just be patient with your new slow cooker while you're getting used to it—I promise you it's worth it.

Also note that smaller slow cookers can tolerate a greater range of food volume, meaning you can fill these little beauties up more (or less) than larger slow cookers, which typically require filling to ½ to ¾ capacity. This is because smaller cookers hold less volume overall, so their heat distribution is more even and consistent. I've filled mine ⅞ full, and even halfway or less (when baking a cookie), and it works every time!

I can't state strongly enough, however, that learning how your slow cooker works is the key to making a great meal. It's worth your time and effort, and you will be rewarded with many breakfasts and dinners waiting for you.

Cook While You Are Away from Home or Even Asleep

Some people are reluctant to leave any electrical appliance plugged in while they are away from home. I cook most days using one of my slow cookers while I'm away at work and when I'm sleeping, too. That way I can wake up to a wholesome breakfast and come home to a ready-to-eat dinner. I have never had a problem with any of my 20-plus slow cookers (both old and new), but there are a few things that you can do to ease your mind.

Always make sure the area around the slow cooker and its cord is clear. The outside of the slow cooker is metal and should never come into contact with paper or other combustibles. You also want to make sure it's out of reach of little hands or paws. The metal sides get hot enough to burn delicate fingers.

Most slow cookers have feet that separate the hot body from the countertop. The best way to leave nothing to chance is to place a trivet under the slow cooker. Depending on the type of countertop you have, you may want to double up on the trivets or put the trivet on top of a pot holder. That way, if your slow cooker gets really hot, your counter won't be damaged.

I have never damaged a counter myself, but a cookbook author friend of mine, Debbie Moose, told me a slow cooker melted hers. So it's better to be safe than sorry.

When you buy a new slow cooker, you should always stay at home the first time you cook in it. That way if there is a defect, you'll be there to catch it. It's a good idea to do this with any appliances that involve heat.

NOTE: COOKING TIMES FOR THE RECIPES

Most of the recipes in this book cook for 7 to 9 hours. But some of the recipes cook in 1½ to 3 hours. The quicker cooking times are best for weekends, holidays, or evenings when you can wait an hour or two for dinner. Most of the pastas fall into this category because by their nature they cook fast. Many of the desserts cook in shorter times, too, which allows you to start them just before dinner so they are ready when you are. Cooking times are marked in each recipe for you to be able to pick these out.

Cooking Longer than 8 or 9 Hours

There are some short cooking recipes in this book, but the majority are written just so you can stay away the entire workday, or about 8 or 9 hours.

Once you're used to using your slow cooker, you'll realize about how much liquid you need to add for an extra hour or two of cooking time. Also, pick well: a soup or stew will be one of the easiest ways for you to get to know how your slow cooker cooks. Plus, there's no need to be worried about your dinner burning because there is already a lot of liquid involved.

I've cooked many of the recipes for as long as 10 to 12 hours with great success and just a little extra liquid.

Make Cleanup a Snap

It's not difficult to remove even the most baked-on food from your slow cooker. How simple is it? Wait until your crock cools off, fill it with soapy water, and let it soak overnight or all day. Most foods will come right off (especially burnt-on oatmeal) in one piece. You may have to use a scrubby to get every last bit, but it's still pretty easy.

If this approach doesn't work, you may have to soak the crock a second time.

A preventive method is to use a square of parchment paper to line the slow cooker—similar to how you'd press a square of paper into a muffin tin. Then you can throw the paper away instead of washing up. This won't work well with soups or watery stews, but the cleanup for those is already super-easy.

Note: I'm not keen on lining the crock with a slow cooker cooking bag. I don't like the cost or the idea of cooking in plastic. Although they're not necessary, you are welcome to use them if you want to.

PRECOOK ONIONS THE EASY WAY

There are two kinds of people in the world—those who think you should sauté onions before you put them into the slow cooker to make the flavor better and those who don't think you should have to sauté anything when you are cooking in a slow cooker.

If you have my first book, *The Vegan Slow Cooker*, you know I think it's worth the time to sauté. However, in this book, I've tried to think of an easier way. So make sure to check out the recipe on page 19 for Ahead-of-the-Game Big Batch of Cooked Onions, so you can make a batch in the slow cooker one day and use them whenever you need. You get a great flavor by cooking onions this way because it really brings out their sweetness. A batch may last you a few weeks, and you can freeze them in ice cube trays just like bouillon so nothing is wasted.

TIPS AND TRICKS FOR COOKING FOR SMALL FAMILIES

It's easy to get dinner on the table every night when you plan well. This is true in a large family or small one. But the great thing is that taking 30 minutes to an hour each week to plan can save you hundreds of dollars and hours of time.

If you go to the grocery store at least once a week, planning won't take much time from your already hectic schedule. It took a long time for me to get on board the planning train, but I love saving time. You'll use up the food you buy because it's all written down and avoid those last-minute trips to the grocery during its busiest time.

Because these recipes are for small amounts, you may not use a whole package of tofu or tempeh—even a can of beans or tomatoes might be more than you need. When this happens, you have a few choices. 1. Plan your meals so you'll use the remainder up within the week. 2. Freeze the extras for the next time you'll need them. 3. Take it to the compost pile feeling a bit miffed with yourself for wasting food.

I was a number 3er for a long time. I can tell you just how much I hate the walk of shame to the compost bin. (At least it's better than the trash . . .) But these days, I practice a combination of planning and freezing. You'll see more helpful freezing tips on the next page. The most important thing is not to fool yourself into thinking you'll use something before it goes bad because you probably won't. That alone will save you trips to the store and money.

Menu Planning 101

To get started, try to set aside one 15- to 30-minute session a week to think about your meal plan. If it helps to make it fun, go on pinterest.com and search for printable menu plans. There are tons of prettified menu plans that you can print out and place on your table while you plan for the week ahead. It's always easier for me to get in an organizing frame of mind when I have a form to fill out, and having pretty ones makes it fun. It's best to do this a day or so before you go grocery shopping or to the market. If you have a CSA share, your plans may be up in the air a little because you may not know what you're getting until your box of goodies arrives. I've suggested substitutions for many of the recipes so you can use ingredients that are right in season.

While you're planning meals, take note of the use of half a package of tofu or tempeh and go ahead and add another recipe to use it up in the same week. Feel free to always substitute local seasonal ingredients for those called for in a recipe. Swapping turnips for potatoes, collards for kale, or winter squash for summer squash will change the recipes a little, but it will also guarantee you the freshest-tasting ingredients. Cooking with the seasons is one of the best ways to trim your budget because in-season veggies are always cheaper, and they taste the best, too.

Use Your Freezer All Year Long

Whether it's making Ahead-of-the-Game Big Batch of Cooked Onions (page 19) or freezing leftover tomato paste into tablespoon-sized (15 g) splotches on aluminum foil, your freezer will save you time and money.

Don't forget that you can freeze green peppers, summer squash, green beans, and more when they are in season. Having a summer meal on a snowy day can be just the thing that lifts the winter blues. Herbs freeze well when puréed with olive oil or water, and like most things, they freeze well in ice cube trays for the perfect portion to drop into a soup or stew.

Most of the recipes and their leftovers will freeze well, so if you are single, you don't have to eat the same meal more than once a week unless you want to. Just freeze it for another meal, perhaps for a day that you would've eaten out instead of cooking.

NEW-TO-YOU INGREDIENTS

If you are new to vegan eating or certain ethnic cuisines, you may find yourself introduced to a few unfamiliar ingredients in this book. I've compiled some tips and tricks below for fitting new spices into your meals and budget, info to help you pick the right nondairy milk for your recipes, and some details on some typical vegan foods including tofu, tempeh, and seitan.

Spices. If you can, buy spices in the bulk bins. You can find them in most health food stores and some regular groceries. They are typically cheaper and fresher than those sold in jars or containers. Also, you can buy as little as a teaspoon at a time and then, if the spice isn't to your liking, you won't need to throw any out. However, if you find yourself loving it, you can buy more of it next time.

Even if you aren't in a metropolis, you can get any of the spices in these recipes online. Check out the resources in the back of this book. You can get a wide variety of spices inexpensively and delivered right to your door. Before you know it, you'll be serving up international dishes that taste as good as those in your favorite restaurants.

Nondairy milk. There are milks made with soy, rice, coconut, almond, hazelnut, hemp, and oats—the list grows longer every month as new ones pop up. In addition, these varieties come sweetened; sweetened and flavored; unsweetened; unsweetened and flavored; and plain. In case you're new to nondairy milks, here are a few facts to get you started.

- Plain milks typically contain sweeteners but no other flavors like vanilla or chocolate.

- Unsweetened milk has no added sweetener, but it may have some sweetness that naturally comes from the base ingredient.

- Flavored milks come both sweetened and unsweetened.

- Unsweetened and unflavored is my favorite type to cook with because it allows the flavors of the dish to stand out.

- Almond milk has a mild flavor and is fairly thin. The unsweetened vanilla is my personal favorite in oatmeal.

- Choose an appropriate nondairy milk in accordance with your diet or dietary restrictions.

- Coconut milk from a carton is a little thinner than from a can and does not have a strong coconut flavor. Unsweetened coconut milk is my favorite to use in savory soups and stews.

- Hazelnut milk has a light hazelnut flavor. Chocolate hazelnut milk can transform your plain coffee into a Nutella coffee in just one pour.

- Oat milk is thick and fairly sweet. It's good in coffee and breakfast dishes.

- Rice milk is the thinnest of the nondairy milks and has a slight sweetness even if you get the unsweetened version.

- Soy milk is usually one of the first nondairy milks people try. Each brand tastes different, with some being more beany tasting than others.

- There are also nondairy creamers made with nuts, soy, or coconut. These are pretty sweet, so make adjustments in any sugar or sweeteners that are called for in a recipe. (You can also make your own with recipes from this book!)

Meat alternatives. If you are making a lifestyle change or just adding a few new meatless meals into your rotation, here is a quick introduction to some of the healthy proteins that are often used in vegan cuisine.

Seitan is sometimes called wheat meat or wheat gluten. If you've ever made bread and noticed the strands that form while you're kneading—that's gluten. In the old days, before wheat gluten flour was plentiful, people would make a dough and rinse it under warm water until all that was left was the gluten. Now, it's as easy as mixing wheat gluten flour with water! It has a dense texture that's a little chewy and is a protein element to add to a dish and easy to make in your slow cooker. If you don't feel like making it yourself, you can always substitute store-bought seitan. (Upton's is one of my favorite brands.) You can make a lot of recipes you grew up with by using seitan in place of any meat. Also, it's much cheaper if you make it yourself.

However, if you have a gluten allergy, seitan is not for you. But you can substitute pressed firm tofu in many of the recipes for seitan. And you can substitute seitan for tofu or tempeh if you're avoiding foods that contain soy.

Tempeh and tofu. I love tofu and tempeh and find that they can easily be the main events in your meal. Some people avoid these soy-containing foods for various reasons. If you're like me and trying to avoid GMOs (genetically modified organisms), buy organic soy products or those clearly labeled that they aren't made from GMO soybeans.

Tofu has the texture of soft cheese, so for most of the recipes you will press it beforehand to make it firmer. Pressing it is easy. Just wrap it in clean dish towels, place on a cutting board, and put a cast-iron pan on top for 20 minutes to an hour. This removes the water from it, making it firmer and better able to soak up flavors in a marinade or sauce.

You can marinate the pressed tofu ahead of time, but often cooking all day in the slow cooker works just as well to infuse it with flavors.

There are different kinds of tofu, including silken, soft, firm, and extra-firm. Silken tofu has a smooth texture that works great in desserts, spreads, and dips, but it isn't suited to pressing. Most recipes call for firm tofu, but you can use soft tofu and just press it for longer.

Like tofu, tempeh is made of soy, but it has a firmer, denser texture and contains split soybeans. Another difference is that tempeh is made using a culture and is fermented, making it easier to digest than other soy foods. It can taste a bit bitter to some people. If you're in that group, try steaming it for 10 to 15 minutes before you cook it. You can even do this in advance and freeze it for later.

I've found a great local tempeh maker, and the culture she uses creates a nonbitter tempeh. I'd recommend that you look around for one in your area.

Grains. In this book, I use a wide variety of grains including steel-cut oats, barley, oat groats, and others. Like spices, these are cheaper when you buy them from the bulk bins. Also, you can order them online if some of them are not available where you live.

If you don't have the particular grain called for, try a different one. Just remember that brown rice and quinoa will break down some if cooked all day while oat groats, barley, and some other grains will stay more solid. Go ahead and experiment your heart out!

CHAPTER TWO

BUDGET RESCUERS:
EASY DIY STAPLES

MORE PEOPLE ARE PAYING ATTENTION to what goes into the food they bring home from the store. Making your own staples, however, puts you in the driver's seat. You can leave out spices your family doesn't like, only use organic ingredients, and best of all, you know exactly what you're feeding your family!

Which brings me to this chapter—my favorite chapter in every book I've written. I love re-creating some of my most-used ingredients from scratch to cut my food budget. These recipes can be made once and used in several recipes, so it's worth the effort. However, if you're more short on time than money, feel free to substitute store-bought items.

The Nut Ricotta makes a great spread on pizzas in addition to being a star in the Hearty Lasagna Layered with Nut Ricotta (page 25). And Monika's Grain-Based Italian Sausages (page 17) are a versatile addition to many of your favorite recipes.

ITALIAN SEITAN COINS

★ SOY-FREE   ★ OIL-FREE

My picky eater likes to have some hearty dishes with seitan and tempeh in our weekly menu rotation. Premade seitan can be expensive, and in some places it can be hard to find. However, it's easy to make yourself and then you can control all the ingredients that go in it! Use this as a base recipe when making other sausages. Just vary the spice blend to make chorizo, breakfast sausage, and more.

FOR THE BROTH:

3 cups (700 ml) water

2 vegan bouillon cubes

FOR THE SEITAN:

1 cup (120 g) vital wheat gluten flour

1 teaspoon tomato paste

1 teaspoon dried basil

1 teaspoon dried thyme

1 teaspoon dried marjoram

½ teaspoon black pepper

½ teaspoon paprika

½ teaspoon onion powder (or 1 teaspoon puréed sautéed onion)

¼ teaspoon cayenne or other hot pepper powder

¼ teaspoon dried ground rosemary or ½ teaspoon fresh rosemary

¼ teaspoon salt or salt substitute

¾ cup (175 ml) water

Add the water and bouillon cubes to the slow cooker and cook on high while preparing the seitan.

Put all the seitan ingredients except for the water into a food processor and process until well combined. Add half the water, process until absorbed, and then add the rest. It may not completely combine. Scrape the seitan mixture onto a cutting board and knead for about 5 minutes (or use your food processor or bread maker to save your wrists). Cut the ball of seitan dough into 8 pieces and roll them into logs. You may have to knead each piece for a few minutes before they come together to make a nice shape.

Cut the seitan into coins now instead of after they are cooked—it will make them cook faster, and they will already be in the shape called for in the recipes.

Place all the seitan coins in the slow cooker with the broth. Cook until the pieces start to rise up, about 2 to 3 hours. (You will keep the temperature turned to high.) If they are a little heavy, they will not float. Store in the fridge or freezer with their broth.

YIELD: 1½ cups (355 ml) or enough to use in 2 recipes

PER ½-CUP (120 ML) SERVING: 149.5 calories; 0.7 g total fat; 0.1 g saturated fat; 30.1 g protein; 5.9 g carbohydrate; 0.3 g dietary fiber; 0 mg cholesterol

PREP TIME: 15 minutes

COOKING TIME: 2 to 3 hours

MONIKA'S GRAIN-BASED ITALIAN SAUSAGES

★ SOY-FREE   ★ GLUTEN-FREE   ★ OIL-FREE OPTION*

Monika Soria Caruso, my good friend and gluten-free vegan recipe developer, comes to the rescue again, as she has in the past when I needed gluten-free versions of recipes. Monika advises that any gluten-free meat substitute, like this one, can be added to a dish no more than 5 minutes before serving without falling apart. Check her other gluten-free goodies at her blog, windycityvegan.wordpress.com.

½ cup (100 g) cooked brown lentils, drained

2 teaspoons (10 g) tomato paste

1 teaspoon each garlic powder, dried basil, dried thyme, and dried oregano or marjoram

½ teaspoon onion powder

½ teaspoon kosher salt

½ teaspoon ground black pepper

½ cup (98 g) cold, cooked long-grain brown rice

½ cup (93 g) cold, cooked quinoa

¾ cup (84 g) almond meal

¼ cup (24 g) nutritional yeast flakes

Preheat oven to 350°F (180°C, or gas mark 4) and place a rack in the center position. Line a baking tray with parchment paper* or oil lightly.

In a food processor, purée the first nine ingredients (through pepper) into a paste. Transfer to a large mixing bowl and set aside.

In the same food processor (no need to wash between steps), combine the grains, almond meal, and nutritional yeast. Pulse until coarsely ground but not puréed.

Add the rice mixture to the lentil mixture and stir until everything is completely incorporated. It will have the texture of veggie loaf. Wet your hands and shape into links or meatballs. Space evenly on the tray at least 1 inch (2.5 cm) apart.

If making links: Bake for 10 minutes, flip your links over, and bake for an additional 10 minutes. Turn the oven off, leave the tray inside for 10 more minutes, and then remove the tray and allow to cool at room temperature.

If making meatballs: bake for 10 minutes, flip over, and bake for an additional 10 minutes. Remove the tray and allow to cool at room temperature.

YIELD: about 30 links or meatballs
PER 1-MEATBALL SERVING: 41.5 calories; 2.0 g total fat; 0.1 g saturated fat; 2.0 g protein; 4.6 g carbohydrate; 1.1 g dietary fiber; 0 mg cholesterol
PREP TIME: 15 minutes
COOKING TIME: 20 to 30 minutes

RECIPE VARIATION
These links or meatballs can easily be simmered in a red sauce for a couple of minutes before dressing pasta; sliced in half and used to top a pizza before baking; or tucked into a baked pasta dish the last few minutes the dish bakes until heated through.

MAKE-YOUR-OWN GLUTEN CRUMBLES

★ SOY-FREE   ★ OIL-FREE

I know many people avoid store-bought seitan and faux meat. Instead, you can easily make these crumbles at home so that you'll know every ingredient that went into them. Unlike many commercial crumbles, there is no soy in these.

1 cup (235 ml) vegan broth

¾ cup (175 ml) water

1 cup (120 g) vital wheat gluten flour

½ teaspoon each powdered ginger, thyme, oregano, and smoked paprika

¼ to ½ teaspoon each salt and pepper

¼ teaspoon dried ground rosemary or ½ teaspoon fresh rosemary

¼ teaspoon ground coriander

¼ teaspoon onion powder or 1 teaspoon puréed fresh onion

¼ teaspoon granulated garlic or 2 minced garlic cloves

Add the broth to your slow cooker and turn on high. Let it warm up a bit while you make the gluten.

Put the rest of the ingredients in a mixer or food processor and combine. They will be pretty moist after mixed, but you should still be able to make a free-form loaf out of them. Wrap the loaf securely in foil. Even if the water isn't warm yet, add the wrapped loaf to the slow cooker and cook for 3 to 4 hours.

Carefully open some of the aluminum foil with tongs and peek at it; you don't want the edges to be too dried out, but they should be firm. Cook for another 30 to 60 minutes if you feel it's not quite done.

After the loaf is done cooking, remove, unwrap, and let cool. Then cut it into chunks and put into your food processor. Process until it looks like crumbles. Use like you would other crumbles in chili, tacos, etc.

YIELD: about 2 cups (220 g)
PER ½-CUP (55 G) SERVING: 149.5 calories; 0.7 g total fat; 0.1 g saturated fat; 30.1 g protein; 5.9 g carbohydrate; 0.3 g dietary fiber; 0 mg cholesterol
PREP TIME: 15 minutes
COOKING TIME: 3 to 5 hours

RECIPE VARIATION
Change the spices to suit your recipes. Try using cumin and your favorite ground chiles for a Mexican flavor or even sausage spices like sage, marjoram, oregano, rosemary, smoked paprika, coriander, and garlic.

AHEAD-OF-THE-GAME BIG BATCH OF COOKED ONIONS

★ SOY-FREE   ★ GLUTEN-FREE   ★ OIL-FREE OPTION*

The onions called for in the recipes are supposed to be precooked because I find that cooking them before they go into the slow cooker produces a deeper flavor and in turn, a better-tasting dish. Some people think all slow-cooked dishes taste alike, but precooking your onions is the first step away from that sameness. Of course, using a variety of spices and reseasoning the dish before serving it also ensures a tasty meal that doesn't blend in with the one before it. However, I can't think of anyone who really likes or has the time for frequently sautéing onions a tablespoon (10 g) or two at a time. At first, I thought the answer was to sauté a big batch on the stovetop and freeze them in small amounts for later use. But I find that cooking a large batch in the slow cooker takes less effort and bother. I think you'll love this method as much as I do!

About 3 medium onions, or enough to fill your small slow cooker ¾ of the way full, minced or diced (your choice)

1 to 2 tablespoons (15 to 28 ml) olive oil or ¼ cup (60 ml) water*

½ teaspoon salt, optional

Oil your slow cooker or *use water to make the recipe oil-free.

Add all the ingredients to your slow cooker and cook on low for 7 to 9 hours. Once cool, put the amount you'll use in the next 5 days in a container in the fridge. Freeze the rest in ice cube trays in 1 tablespoon (10 g) measurements.

YIELD: 3 to 4 cups (261 to 348 g)

PER 1-TABLESPOON (5.4 G) SERVING: 4.4 calories; 0.3 g total fat; 0 g saturated fat; 0.1 g protein; 0.5 g carbohydrate; 0.1 g dietary fiber; 0 mg cholesterol

PREP TIME: 15 minutes

COOKING TIME: 7 to 9 hours

BOLD LEMON PEAR SPREAD

★ GLUTEN-FREE   ★ OIL-FREE   ★ SOY-FREE OPTION*

Although the color of this spread is a subdued mauve, the brilliant, sharp lemon flavor it packs more than makes up for it. The optional silken tofu makes it thicker, but it still spreads wonderfully on a scone without it.

2 cups (322 g) peeled, chopped pears

¼ cup (60 ml) lemon juice

Sweetener of your choice, to taste (I use ½ teaspoon stevia.)

1 teaspoon lemon extract

1 teaspoon arrowroot

¼ cup (60 g) silken tofu, optional (*omit for soy-free)

In the morning: Add the pears and lemon juice to the slow cooker and cook on low for 7 to 9 hours.

When you get home, put the cooked mixture in a food processor with the rest of the ingredients and process until smooth. Store in the fridge for up to 2 weeks.

YIELD: about 2 cups (640 g)

PER 1-TABLESPOON (20 G) SERVING: 6.7 calories; 0.1 g total fat; 0 g saturated fat; 0.2 g protein; 1.5 g carbohydrate; 0.3 g dietary fiber; 0 mg cholesterol

PREP TIME: 15 minutes

COOKING TIME: 7 to 9 hours

RECIPE VARIATION
Try making different spreads by varying the extract and juice. Lavender extract and lemon juice = yum!

SAMBAR SPICE POWDER

★ SOY-FREE ★ GLUTEN-FREE
★ OIL-FREE OPTION*

Many Indian dishes have split peas or beans as a seasoning. This blend uses split baby chickpeas, or channa dal. Urad dal, skinned and split black lentils, is used in many dishes as well and lends a peanutty taste even though it doesn't contain nuts.

3 tablespoons (47 g) channa dal

1 teaspoon olive oil (*use a nonstick pan to make oil-free)

3 tablespoons (15 g) coriander seeds

3 teaspoons (11 g) mustard seeds

2 teaspoons (4 g) cumin seeds

2 teaspoons (4 g) fenugreek seeds

4 to 8 dried red chile peppers

Soak the channa dal in ½ cup (120 ml) of water for about 5 minutes while you measure out the other spices, and then drain in a strainer.

Heat the olive oil over medium heat in a large pan. Add the rest of the ingredients, including the drained dal, and sauté for a few minutes until the spices begin to smell stronger, a sign that you've released the oils.

Remove the from pan and grind in a spice or coffee grinder (or a very strong food processor or blender) until a coarse powder is formed.

YIELD: about ⅓ cup (60 g)
PREP TIME: 15 minutes
COOKING TIME: none

GARAM MASALA

★ SOY-FREE ★ GLUTEN-FREE ★ OIL-FREE

This is a traditional blend of spices that varies in each Indian home. Use this recipe as a starting point and change up the ingredients to suit your fancy.

¼ cup (20 g) coriander seeds

10 cardamom pods

1 tablespoon (5 g) peppercorns

2 teaspoons (4 g) cumin seeds

1 to 2 cinnamon sticks

4 whole cloves

3 bay leaves

Toast all the spices in a nonstick pan over mediumn heat until they become fragrant, about 5 to 10 minutes. Grind in a spice or coffee grinder. Store in an airtight container.

YIELD: about ½ cup (56 g)
PREP TIME: 15 minutes
COOKING TIME: none

RECIPE VARIATIONS

- Don't have whole spices? Use ground spices, but watch carefully while toasting them because they will be ready much earlier and burn more quickly. Having ground bay leaf on hand makes these spice blends a snap because they can take so long to grind.
- Try this spice blend on some freshly popped popcorn or in a savory oatmeal. Even a pinch in your hot chocolate will make life a little spicier.

BERBERE SPICE MIX

★ SOY-FREE   ★ GLUTEN-FREE   ★ OIL-FREE

This delicious blend of spices breathes life into boring veggies. Use it in the Ethiopian Style Tempeh W'et and Veggie Meal (page 148), but also try it any time you need to spice things up. Berbere is similar to a curry blend, but the traditional blend is extra-spicy. The heat in this one is lowered for non-Ethiopian taste buds, but you can make it hotter or milder as you wish.

2 tablespoons (14 g) paprika

1 tablespoon (5.3 g) cayenne pepper

1 teaspoon ground fenugreek

1 teaspoon ground ginger

½ teaspoon cardamom

½ teaspoon coriander

½ teaspoon black pepper

½ teaspoon nutmeg

¼ teaspoon cinnamon

¼ teaspoon allspice

¼ teaspoon cloves

Mix together in a small bowl and store in an airtight container.

YIELD: about ¼ cup (28 g)
PREP TIME: 5 minutes
COOKING TIME: none

ITALIAN SEASONING

★ SOY-FREE   ★ GLUTEN-FREE   ★ OIL-FREE

This is just a simple blend I like to have on hand. It's just so easy to grab when you need to infuse some Italian flavors in a pinch. Marjoram and oregano are close relatives and are often used interchangeably. Try smelling them side by side to detect their subtle differences. I find that marjoram has a heady, almost flowery note to it while oregano is a bit bolder. They both add their specialness to this versatile spice blend.

1 tablespoon (2 g) dried basil

1 tablespoon (3 g) dried oregano

1 tablespoon (1.7 g) dried marjoram

1 tablespoon (2.7 g) dried thyme

1 teaspoon dried rosemary or ½ teaspoon ground rosemary

Add everything to a food processor and process until uniform, about 1 minute. Store in an airtight jar.

YIELD: about ⅓ cup (24 g)
PREP TIME: 5 minutes
COOKING TIME: none

RECIPE VARIATION

To make the easiest pasta sauce ever, add 1 or 2 tablespoons (4.5 or 9 g) of Italian Seasoning to a can of crushed or puréed tomatoes—perfect when it's just before payday and the cupboard is bare or you need a just-from-the-pantry meal.

CAJUN SPICE BLEND

★ SOY-FREE   ★ GLUTEN-FREE   ★ OIL-FREE

You can buy a Cajun blend in the store, but most of them contain a ton of salt.
This is a salt-free blend that's budget-friendly, too.

2 teaspoons (5 g) paprika

2 teaspoons (2.8 g) dried thyme

1 teaspoon dried oregano

1 teaspoon dried marjoram

1 bay leaf or ½ teaspoon ground
bay leaf

½ teaspoon cayenne pepper

½ teaspoon onion powder

½ teaspoon granulated garlic

½ teaspoon lemon zest

¼ teaspoon black pepper

⅛ teaspoon allspice

⅛ teaspoon cloves

Grind everything together in a spice mill for 2 to 5 minutes until the mixture is smooth or for about 10 minutes in a small food processor. It's very important that the bay leaf get ground into a powder. If you don't have a spice grinder, you can buy ground bay leaf to use in this recipe.

YIELD: a little less than a ¼ cup (28 g)
PREP TIME: 15 minutes
COOKING TIME: none

DID YOU KNOW?
Cajun food isn't typically super-hot and spicy, but you can make this blend spicier or milder to agree with your family's taste buds.

SMALL BATCH DRY BEANS

★ SOY-FREE   ★ GLUTEN-FREE   ★ OIL-FREE

Making beans in the slow cooker is super-simple. No soaking is necessary, but if you prefer to soak them, be my guest. Take note that some of the recipes in this book use precooked beans and others call for cooking them with the dish. If you don't use the whole batch of beans, you can always freeze them for later.

1 cup (250 g) dried beans (other than lentils or kidney beans)

3 cups (700 ml) water

Add beans and water to slow cooker. Cook on low 8 to 10 hours. When you come home, your beans will be ready for you to use in another recipe. You may have extra water in the beans. Simply drain them in a colander if you don't want to use the broth.

YIELD: between 2½ to 3 cups (250 to 300 g) depending on the bean
PREP TIME: 5 minutes
COOKING TIME: 8 to 10 hours

RECIPE VARIATION

If you already know what kind of dish you'll be using your beans for, you could get a head start by throwing in some spices while they are cooking. Try cumin for a Mexican flavor, Italian seasoning, or even some garam masala. Just don't add fresh herbs because the flavors will cook out before you add the beans to your recipe.

DID YOU KNOW?

You can use kidney beans, but you must boil them for a full 10 minutes on the stove before adding to the slow cooker. This is because kidney beans contain a toxic agent, phytohemagglutinin, also known as kidney bean lectin, but the boiling eliminates any danger.

NUT RICOTTA

★ SOY-FREE   ★ GLUTEN-FREE   ★ OIL-FREE

This recipe takes minutes to make and can turn a plain lasagna into
something amazing. Even though it has no added oil, it is not low in fat because
of all the nuts, so keep that in mind if you are following a special diet.

1 cup (235 ml) water

1 cup (140 g) cashews

½ cup (55 g) slivered almonds

¼ cup (35 g) macadamia nuts

2 teaspoons (10 ml) lemon juice

1 teaspoon apple cider vinegar

½ to 1 teaspoon salt, to taste

EXTRAS:

¼ cup (10 g) fresh basil

1 or 2 cloves fresh garlic

1 teaspoon dried oregano

1 teaspoon chives (fresh or dried)

1 to 2 tablespoons (6 to 12 g)
nutritional yeast flakes

Put all the ingredients except for any extras you plan on using in the
food processor and process until fairly smooth, but not as smooth as
nut butter.

Add any extras you desire and process a bit more until mixed in. Store
in the fridge for up to a week. Use in lasagna, pastas, or as a spread on
sandwiches or crackers.

YIELD: about 2½ cups (650 g)

PER ¼-CUP (65 G) SERVING: 134.6 calories; 11.5 g total fat; 1.8 g saturated fat;
3.7 g protein; 6.3 g carbohydrate; 1.2 g dietary fiber; 0 mg cholesterol

PREP TIME: 10 minutes

COOKING TIME: none

RECIPE VARIATION

If your blender isn't very strong, you can soak the nuts overnight or
even cook them covered with water for about 15 minutes. Then even
the wimpiest blender can make them creamy.

DID YOU KNOW?

The higher fat content in nuts makes them ideal for dairy
substitutes, such as in this ricotta recipe, the sour cream substitute
(Cashew Cream on page 28), and as part of the easiest Creamy
Tomato Basil Bisque (page 75).

GOLDEN VEGGIE BOUILLON POWDER

★ SOY-FREE ★ GLUTEN-FREE ★ OIL-FREE

I typically make my bouillon and freeze the extras to use later. But what if you have no room in the freezer or if you want to take some camping? This powder is your answer. It stores in your spice cabinet and you just use 2 tablespoons (14 g) to substitute for 1 bouillon cube.

1 cup (96 g) nutritional yeast flakes

2 tablespoons (5.4 g) dried thyme

1 tablespoon (1.3 g) dried parsley

1 tablespoon (7 g) onion powder

1 teaspoon paprika

Add everything to your food processor and blend until uniform. Use 2 tablespoons (14 g) bouillon powder wherever a recipe in the book calls for a bouillon cube.

YIELD: ¼ cup (28 g)
PREP TIME: 10 minutes
COOKING TIME: none

RECIPE VARIATION

Make a quick cheezy herb sauce by mixing some Golden Veggie Bouillon Powder into a little warm water. Start with 2 tablespoons (14 g) of the powder and add 1 tablespoon (15 ml) water and then keep adding water, 1 teaspoon at a time, until it's as thin or as thick as you like. In serving over steamed broccoli, thin with the cooking water to capture the extra vitamins.

MIX-AND-MATCH BOUILLON

★ SOY-FREE   ★ GLUTEN-FREE   ★ OIL-FREE OPTION*

This bouillon is slightly different than my other bouillon recipes because you have more freedom to change up the ingredients. In addition to the onion and carrot, add a few of your favorite herbs and veggies to the mix. Avoid veggies in the cabbage family because they will overpower your bouillon.

1 large onion, cut into quarters

2 medium carrots, chopped

½ cup (120 ml) water

OPTIONAL INGREDIENTS
(PICK TWO OR THREE):

2 sprigs fresh thyme or 1 teaspoon dried thyme

2 sprigs fresh parsley or 1 teaspoon dried parsley

1 sprig fresh rosemary

2 stalks celery, chopped

1 cup (156 g) diced celery root

1 cup (140 g) diced winter squash

½ cup (90 g) diced tomatoes

½ teaspoon pepper or to taste

1 teaspoon salt

½ cup (48 g) nutritional yeast flakes

Add the onion, carrot, and water with a few of the optional ingredients you'd like to use in the slow cooker. Note that if you're using nutritional yeast, it will be blended in after cooking and not added in this step. Cook on low 8 to 12 hours. You can spray the empty slow cooker with oil before adding your ingredients, or *use the water to keep the veggies from sticking to the crock.

After cooking, remove any fresh herb stems if you used them. Add the contents of the crock and the optional nutritional yeast to a blender or food processor. If using a blender, always purée in small batches of about 2 to 3 cups at a time because if the blender is too full, the hot liquid might push the lid off.

Freeze bouillon in ice cube trays with 2 tablespoons (28 ml) in each cube. (The average ice cube tray holds about 2 tablespoons [28 ml].)

I typically use 1 to 2 tablespoons (15 to 28 ml) of store-bought bouillon when a recipe calls for 1 veggie bouillon cube, so that works out to 2 to 4 tablespoons (28 to 45 ml) of this recipe or about 1 to 2 ice cubes.

YIELD: 1½ to 2 cups (355 ml to 475 ml) bouillon
PER 2-TABLESPOON (28 ML) SERVING: 15.6 calories; 0.1 g total fat; 0 g saturated fat; 1.2 g protein; 2.7 g carbohydrate; 0.7 g dietary fiber; 0 mg cholesterol
PREP TIME: 10 minutes
COOKING TIME: 8 to 12 hours

CASHEW CREAM

★ GLUTEN-FREE ★ OIL-FREE
★ SOY-FREE

Some people love the convenience of store-bought vegan sour cream but don't like the soy that is in some of them. Cashew cream is a great soy-free solution that can be hard to find but easy to make. It makes soups and stews thick and rich. I think you'll love it!

---

1 cup (145 g) cashews
¼ to ½ cup (60 to 120 ml) water
Juice of 1 lemon

Add cashews, ¼ cup (60 ml) water, and lemon juice to a food processor or blender and blend until smooth, scraping down the sides as you go. Add the additional ¼ cup (60 ml) water if you need to thin the mixture or if you have a less powerful blender.

If you are using a food processor, it will take longer than you think to get a smooth mixture. The cashew cream will not be quite as silky smooth as if you had used a powerful blender, but it will still taste great!

YIELD: about 1¼ cups (290 g)
PER 2-TABLESPOON (30 G) SERVING: 49.2 calories; 5.2 g total fat; 1 g saturated fat; 2 g protein; 3.6 g carbohydrate; 0 g dietary fiber; 0 mg cholesterol.
PREP TIME: 5 to 10 minutes
COOKING time: none

EXTRA-THICK SILKEN TOFU SOUR CREAM

★ GLUTEN-FREE ★ OIL-FREE

If you are allergic to nuts and hate buying premade vegan sour creams, this recipe is a perfect solution for you. It's a bonus that it is super-easy to make.

One 12.3-oz (349 g) package silken tofu
1 to 3 tablespoons (15 to 45 ml) water, as needed
Juice of 1 lemon

Add tofu, 1 tablespoon (15 ml) water, and lemon juice to a food processor or blender and blend until smooth, scraping down the sides as you go. Add the additional 1 to 2 tablespoons (15 to 28 ml) water if you need to thin the mixture or if you have a less powerful blender.

YIELD: a little more than 1 cup (230 g)
PER 2-TABLESPOON (30 G) SERVING: 23.1 calories; 1 g total fat; 0 g saturated fat; 1.9 g protein; 1 g carbohydrate; 0 g dietary fiber; 0 mg cholesterol
PREP TIME: 5 minutes
COOKING TIME: none

CHAPTER THREE

MORNING DELIGHTS:
WAKE UP TO BREAKFAST

I HAVE MORE THAN 50 SLOW COOKER OATMEAL RECIPES ON MY BLOG, so I'm known for my love of slow cooker breakfasts. To me, there's nothing better than waking up to a warm bowl of oatmeal—especially with flavors like vanilla fig baklava and coconut banana coffee cake, which make your house smell great, too.

Even if steel-cut oats are your favorite, don't overlook other grains. Many cook up deliciously in the slow cooker, like polenta, barley, oat groats, and quinoa—the list goes on and on. So make sure to add them to your breakfast rotation.

Beyond your morning porridge, there's breakfast hash, scrambled tofu, and best of all, overnight French toast. There are creamers and syrups that allow you to make your favorite coffee drinks at home, which are much cheaper than those sold at big-box coffee chains and don't make you late to work because the line was too long.

PEAR ROSE CARDAMOM OATMEAL

★ SOY-FREE   ★ GLUTEN-FREE   ★ OIL-FREE OPTION*

This oatmeal soothes you with the taste of sweet pears and the fragrances of rosewater and cardamom. It's the perfect oatmeal to pamper yourself with before a big day or after a really hard week.

½ cup (40 g) steel-cut oats

2 cups (475 ml) unsweetened coconut milk (such as So Delicious brand)

1 small pear, chopped

½ teaspoon vanilla extract

½ teaspoon rosewater, food grade

½ teaspoon almond extract

½ teaspoon ground cardamom

¼ teaspoon ground cinnamon

Sweetener of your choice, to taste (I use ¼ teaspoon stevia.)

The night before: Spray your crock with oil to help with cleanup later or skip it* and just plan on soaking your crock immediately afterward so any stuck-on oatmeal will come right off. Add all the ingredients except the sweetener. Cook on low overnight (7 to 9 hours).

In the morning: Stir your oatmeal well and add sweetener. It may seem watery at the top, but when stirred, it should attain a more uniform consistency.

YIELD: about 3 cups (700 g)
PER 1-CUP (233 G) SERVING: 146.7 calories; 5.3 g total fat; 3.7 g saturated fat; 5.3 g protein; 20.0 g carbohydrate; 3.3 g dietary fiber; 0 mg cholesterol
PREP TIME: 10 minutes
COOKING TIME: 7 to 9 hours

RECIPE VARIATION
Try using lavender extract in place of the rosewater. Leave out the cinnamon, and add fresh berries at the end of cooking instead of using pears.

DID YOU KNOW?
When using products like rosewater, check the label for the words "food grade," which means that the product has been certified as safe to ingest. Some rosewater or essences are only suitable for use in perfumes and could contain ingredients that aren't so good for your tummy. The bottle will clearly say "food grade" on the ones you should use.

PUMPKIN CARAMEL BREAKFAST BARLEY

★ SOY-FREE ★ OIL-FREE

Sometimes you have to change up oats for another grain. Trust me, your steel-cut oats will understand. Barley cooks great in the slow cooker while you sleep, and the pumpkin caramel mixed in makes it divine!

½ cup (100 g) barley

2 cups (475 ml) unsweetened nondairy milk

2 to 4 tablespoons (28 to 60 ml) Pumpkin Coconut Caramel Sauce (page 161), to taste

The night before: Add everything but the sauce to the slow cooker and cook on low for 7 to 9 hours.

In the morning: Stir well and then mix in the sauce.

YIELD: about 3 cups (700 g)
PER 1-CUP (233 G) SERVING: 167.5 calories; 3.7 g total fat; 0.9 g saturated fat; 4.1 g protein; 31.9 g carbohydrate; 5.9 g dietary fiber; 0 mg cholesterol
PREP TIME: 10 minutes
COOKING TIME: 7 to 9 hours

CHOCOLATE PUMPKIN BROWNIE BREAKFAST QUINOA

★ SOY-FREE ★ GLUTEN-FREE ★ OIL-FREE

This thick, rich breakfast is a cross between porridge and a pudding. You can even serve it chilled for an extra-healthy dessert in the summer.

2 cups (475 ml) unsweetened nondairy milk

½ cup (87 g) quinoa

½ cup (123 g) pumpkin purée

2 tablespoons (10 g) unsweetened cocoa powder

1 teaspoon vanilla extract

½ teaspoon ground cinnamon

Sweetener of your choice, to taste
(I use ½ teaspoon stevia.)

The night before: Add everything but the sweetener to the slow cooker and cook on low for 7 to 9 hours.

In the morning: Add the sweetener and enjoy this thick chocolate delight.

YIELD: about 3 cups (700 g)
PER 1-CUP (233 G) SERVING: 158.0 calories; 4.4 g total fat; 0 g saturated fat; 5.5 g protein; 25.3 g carbohydrate; 4.5 g dietary fiber; 0 mg cholesterol
PREP TIME: 10 minutes
COOKING TIME: 7 to 9 hours

VANILLA FIG OATMEAL TOPPED WITH BAKLAVA TOPPING

★ SOY-FREE   ★ GLUTEN-FREE   ★ OIL-FREE OPTION*

This is one of my most popular oatmeal recipes on my blog and around the Web.
It's a vanilla oatmeal with flecks of fig and bursts of cardamom and orange flower water.
On top, it's a gooey nutty topping like most oatmeal has never seen.

½ cup (40 g) steel-cut oats

2 cups (475 ml) unsweetened nondairy milk

½ cup (75 g) chopped dried figs

¼ teaspoon ground cardamom

¼ teaspoon orange flower water, food grade, optional

½ vanilla bean, scraped, or 1 teaspoon vanilla extract

FOR THE TOPPING:

1 tablespoon each (8 g) chopped pistachios, (8 g) walnuts, and (8 g) almonds

1 tablespoon (20 g) agave nectar

Pinch cinnamon

The night before: Spray your crock with oil to help with cleanup later or skip it* and just plan on soaking your crock immediately afterward so any stuck-on oatmeal will come right off. Add everything except the topping ingredients to the slow cooker. In a small bowl, mix together the topping ingredients and store in the fridge until the morning. Cook the oatmeal on low for 7 to 9 hours.

In the morning: Stir your oatmeal well. It may seem watery on top, but if stirred, it should become a more uniform consistency. Top each serving with a few teaspoons of the baklava topping, making it as sweet as you like it.

YIELD: about 3 cups (700 g)

PER 1-CUP (233 G) SERVING: 246.5 calories; 6.0 g total fat; 0.4 g saturated fat; 6.5 g protein; 46.8 g carbohydrate; 7.0 g dietary fiber; 0 mg cholesterol

PREP TIME: 10 minutes

COOKING TIME: 7 to 9 hours

DID YOU KNOW?

Your slow cooker is the easiest way to prepare long cooking grains including steel-cut oats, oat groats, and wheat berries. You can even cook some ahead of time and store in the freezer to add to soups and stews.

SCRAMBLED TOFU BREAKFAST BURRITO

★ OIL-FREE OPTION*   ★ GLUTEN-FREE OPTION**

Sometimes even I need a change from oatmeal. Make this burrito filling right before you go to bed, and it will even let you sleep in. (Add extra water if you'll sleep in longer than 9 hours.) If you have leftovers, prep extra burritos and store in fridge or freezer for busy weekday mornings.

1½ cups (258 g) cooked or 1 can (15 ounces, or 425 g) black beans, rinsed and drained

7 ounces (200 g) tofu, crumbled (no need to press)

2 tablespoons (11 g) cooked onion (page 19)

2 tablespoons (19 g) green pepper, minced

¾ cup (175 ml) water

½ teaspoon ground turmeric

¼ teaspoon ground cumin

¼ teaspoon chili powder

¼ teaspoon smoked paprika

Salt and pepper, to taste

4 whole-wheat burrito-sized tortillas (**use gluten-free)

Extras: salsa, vegan sour cream, Cashew Cream (page 28) or *Extra-Thick Silken Tofu Sour Cream (page 28), shredded vegan cheese (*omit to make oil-fee), lettuce, or other fresh veggies

The night before: Add black beans through smoked paprika and cook on low for 7 to 9 hours.

In the morning: Taste and add salt and pepper. If your tortillas are stiff, put them one at a time over the mixture in the slow cooker and steam them into submission.

Spoon ¼ of the mixture onto the tortillas. Add any extras you'd like, roll up, and serve.

YIELD: 4 burritos
PER 1-CUP (220 G) SERVING (WITHOUT BURRITO SHELL): 130.7 calories; 3.3 g total fat; 0.5 g saturated fat; 10.7 g protein; 16.2 g carbohydrate; 5.8 g dietary fiber; 0 mg cholesterol
PREP TIME: 10 minutes
COOKING TIME: 7 to 9 hours

DID YOU KNOW?

The fat and calorie count in burrito shells vary greatly. Check the package before you buy to get the ones that fit into your diet the best. Some of the ones that are marked low-carb actually have the lowest calories.

PUMPKIN POLENTA

★ SOY-FREE   ★ GLUTEN-FREE   ★ OIL-FREE OPTION*

Polenta in one place is yellow grits in another. Both are made from corn and work in this dish. In addition to breakfast, this polenta can be used as a base for sautéed seasonal veggies or a hearty bean stew for lunch or dinner.

2 cups (475 ml) unsweetened nondairy milk

1 cup pumpkin purée (about ½ a 15-ounce [425 g] can)

½ cup (70 g) polenta or yellow grits

2 cloves garlic, minced

1 tablespoon (15 ml) olive oil, optional*

½ teaspoon dried thyme

½ teaspoon dried sage

⅛ teaspoon ground or ¼ teaspoon chopped fresh rosemary

2 to 3 tablespoons (14 to 21 g) vegan shredded cheese, optional*

1 tablespoon (6 g) nutritional yeast flakes

Salt and pepper, to taste

The night before: Add the milk, pumpkin, polenta, garlic, olive oil, if using, and herbs to the slow cooker. Cook on low for 7 to 9 hours.

In the morning: Stir well and add a little more nondairy milk if the mixture is too dry. Add vegan cheese, if using, and nutritional yeast, and stir again. Add salt and pepper, taste, and adjust any herbs as needed.

YIELD: about 4 cups (968 g)

PER 1-CUP (242 G) SERVING (WITHOUT VEGAN CHEESE): 102.5 calories; 2.0 g total fat; 0 g saturated fat; 2.5 g protein; 18.5 g carbohydrate; 3.0 g dietary fiber; 0 mg cholesterol

PREP TIME: 10 minutes

COOKING TIME: 7 to 9 hours

RECIPE VARIATION
Add 1½ cups (269 g) of cooked white beans (or one 15-ounce [425 g] can, rinsed and drained) in the morning to make this a complete anytime meal.

WINTER-SPICED BUTTERNUT SQUASH PECAN FRENCH TOAST

★ SOY-FREE   ★ GLUTEN-FREE OPTION*   ★ OIL-FREE OPTION**

This is the perfect way to use up that stale whole-wheat bread. The bread is transformed into a nutritional breakfast with butternut squash and pecans that anyone will be happy to eat in the morning!

1 cup (235 ml) nondairy milk

2 tablespoons (28 ml) nondairy creamer (**use regular nondairy milk instead)

1 tablespoon (7 g) ground flaxseeds mixed with 2 tablespoons (28 ml) water

½ teaspoon ground cinnamon

¼ teaspoon ground cardamom

¼ teaspoon ground allspice

Pinch ground cloves

½ teaspoon stevia, optional

2½ cups (300 g) stale bread, cut into chunks (*use gluten-free)

1 cup (140 g) peeled butternut squash, finely chopped

¼ cup (28 g) chopped pecans

Maple syrup, for serving

Mix the milk, creamer, flax mixture, spices, and stevia in a medium-sized bowl. Add the bread and let sit for about 5 minutes so it soaks in some of the wet mixture. Then mix in the butternut squash and pecans.

Spray or wipe the crock with oil or **line with a piece of parchment paper as this casserole is likely to stick to wherever the hot spots in your crock are.

Scrape the mixture into your slow cooker and cook on low for 7 to 9 hours. As soon as your slow cooker cools after serving, fill it with soapy water and soak to remove any stubborn cooked-on pieces of food.

YIELD: about 4 cups (1.1 kg)
PER 1-CUP (282 G) SERVING: 380 calories; 9.7 g total fat; 0.6 g saturated fat; 9.5 g protein; 63.4 g carbohydrate; 10.8 g dietary fiber; 0 mg cholesterol
PREP TIME: 10 minutes
COOKING TIME: 7 to 9 hours

RECIPE VARIATION
Try using homemade Vanilla Hazelnut Creamer (page 45).

DID YOU KNOW?
Please note: As with the Wake Up to Bananas Foster for Breakfast (page 42), it's important that the bread be hearty and stale. If it's not, it will not hold its shape and will essentially melt into the mixture. It will taste fine, but it doesn't look nice at all.

OVERNIGHT TOFU ROOT VEGETABLE HASH

★ GLUTEN-FREE ★ OIL-FREE OPTION*

Wake up to a full breakfast of scrambled tofu, potatoes, and other root veggies that you have on hand. I've listed a few to get you started, but let your farmers' market or CSA be your guide.

2 cups (220 g) diced potatoes

1 cup (140 g) diced winter squash or (130 g) carrots

1 cup (156 g) diced celery root or (150 g) turnip

1 tablespoon (15 ml) olive oil, optional*

½ teaspoon paprika

Pinch salt and pepper

½ cup (120 ml) water

1 cup (7 oz, or 200 g) tofu (no need to press)

1 teaspoon Italian Seasoning (page 22)

½ teaspoon kala namak

½ teaspoon turmeric

The night before: Add the root vegetables to the slow cooker and toss with olive oil, if using, paprika, salt, and pepper. Add water. Cook on low for 7 to 9 hours. (Use more water if sleeping 9 hours or more.)

In the morning: In a small bowl mash the tofu with the Italian Seasoning, kala namak, and turmeric. Scrape mixture on top of the root veggies in the slow cooker. Cook for 30 minutes more on high or until the tofu is toasty hot and ready to eat.

YIELD: about 5 cups (1.1 kg)
PER 1-CUP (225 G) SERVING (WITH OIL): 87.1 calories; 3.7 g total fat; 0.4 g saturated fat; 2.5 g protein; 8.3 g carbohydrate; 1.1 g dietary fiber; 0 mg cholesterol
PREP TIME: 15 minutes
COOKING TIME: 7½ to 9½ hours

DID YOU KNOW?
- Big, mature turnips always need to be peeled, but baby turnips and salad turnips can be used as is.
- Kala namak is a salt that's used in Indian cooking and in a lot of vegan cooking, too. It has a high sulfur content, making your tofu really taste like eggs. You can get it cheapest at an Indian grocery or online. It's often called black salt even though it's actually pink!

WAKE UP TO BANANAS FOSTER FOR BREAKFAST

★ SOY-FREE   ★ GLUTEN-FREE OPTION*   ★ OIL-FREE OPTION**

This delicious, over-the-top breakfast is amazingly easy to make. Even better,
it cooks while you sleep and uses leftover bread. Try using Vanilla Hazelnut Creamer (page 45)
for an even more decadent breakfast.

½ cup (120 ml) nondairy milk

2 medium bananas, mashed

¼ cup (60 ml) dark rum or
1 teaspoon rum flavoring

3 tablespoons (45 ml) nondairy
creamer (**use regular nondairy
milk instead)

1 tablespoon (7 g) ground flaxseeds
mixed with 2 tablespoons (28 ml)
water

½ teaspoon ground cinnamon

½ teaspoon stevia, optional

2½ cups (300 g) stale bread, cut
into chunks (*use gluten-free)

Maple syrup, for serving

Mix the milk, bananas, rum, creamer, flax mixture, cinnamon, and stevia, if using, in a medium-sized bowl. Add the bread and let sit for about 5 minutes so it soaks in some of the wet mixture.

Spray or wipe the crock with a little oil or **line with a piece of parchment paper as this casserole is likely to stick to wherever the hot spots in your crock are.

Scrape the mixture into your slow cooker and cook on low for 7 to 9 hours. As soon as your slow cooker cools after serving, fill with soapy water and soak to remove any stubborn cooked-on pieces of food.

YIELD: about 4 cups (1.1 kg)
PER 1-CUP (282 G) SERVING: 292.6 calories; 3.1 g total fat; 0.1 g saturated fat; 9.3 g protein; 50.8 g carbohydrate; 7.1 g dietary fiber; 0 mg cholesterol
PREP TIME: 10 minutes
COOKING TIME: 7 to 9 hours

DID YOU KNOW?
As with the Winter-Spiced Butternut Squash Pecan French Toast (page 39), it's important that the bread be hearty and stale. If it's not, it will not hold its shape and will essentially melt into the mixture. It will taste fine, but it doesn't look nice at all.

VANILLA HAZELNUT CREAMER

★ SOY-FREE ★ GLUTEN-FREE ★ OIL-FREE

You can make this unsweetened or use any sweetener you prefer.
It's super-thick and rich with minimal ingredients and effort.

1½ cups (355 ml) water

1 cup (135 g) whole hazelnuts

½ vanilla bean, cut lengthwise (or double the vanilla extract below)

1 teaspoon vanilla extract

Sweetener of your choice, to taste (I used ¼ teaspoon stevia.)

Pinch or two of salt, optional

Add the water, hazelnuts, and vanilla bean to the slow cooker. Cook on low for 7 to 9 hours.

Carefully pour the cooked mixture into a blender with the vanilla and blend until smooth and creamy. Add sweetener and blend again. Store in the fridge for up to a week.

YIELD: about 2½ cups (570 ml)
PER 1-TABLESPOON (15 ML) SERVING: 26.6 calories; 2.6 g total fat; 0.2 g saturated fat; 0.6 g protein; 0.8 g carbohydrate; 0.4 g dietary fiber; 0 mg cholesterol
PREP TIME: 5 minutes
COOKING TIME: 7 to 9 hours

RECIPE VARIATIONS

- Use other types of nuts you have on hand instead of hazelnuts. You can also use different extracts to change up the flavor.
- You can strain the mixture if you want it silky smooth, but honestly, the thick texture is part of the charm of this creamer.

BLUEBERRY COCONUT COFFEE CREAMER

★ SOY-FREE   ★ GLUTEN-FREE   ★ OIL-FREE

One of my favorite testers requested a flavored coffee creamer,
so this one's for you, Julie. I chose blueberry because it's my picky eater Cheryl's
current favorite. I'm hoping all this gets me extra karma points!

1 can (14 ounces, or 410 ml) light or regular coconut milk

1½ cups whole blueberries, (220g) fresh or (233 g) frozen

½ cup (100 g) sugar

½ vanilla bean, cut in half lengthwise, or 1 teaspoon vanilla extract

1 teaspoon xanthan gum, optional

Add all the ingredients except for the xanthan gum to the slow cooker and cook on low for 7 to 9 hours.

Carefully pour all the ingredients into a blender and blend until smooth. Add the xanthan gum and blend again if you'd like your creamer to be thicker.

YIELD: 2½ to 3 cups (570 to 700 ml)
PER 1-TABLESPOON (15 ML) SERVING: 28.4 calories; 0.9 g total fat; 0.7 g saturated fat; 0.3 g protein; 4.8 g carbohydrate; 0.3 g dietary fiber; 0 mg cholesterol
PREP TIME: 5 minutes
COOKING TIME: 7 to 9 hours

RECIPE VARIATIONS
- If you are avoiding sugar, just substitute your favorite sweetener.
- Try using other fruit like raspberries or even apples to make new creamer combinations.

APPLE CHAI OAT GROATS

★ SOY-FREE   ★ GLUTEN-FREE   ★ OIL-FREE

Steel-cut oats are actually whole oat groats that have been chopped into 2 or 3 pieces.
The taste is the same, but oat groats are denser and a little chewier.

½ cup (92 g) oat groats (Make sure they are clearly marked gluten-free.)

2 cups (475 g) unsweetened nondairy milk

½ cup (125 g) applesauce

½ teaspoon ground cinnamon

½ teaspoon ground cardamom

¼ teaspoon ground allspice

¼ teaspoon ground nutmeg

⅛ teaspoon ground coriander

Pinch ground cloves

Sweetener of your choice, to taste (I use ¼ teaspoon stevia.)

The night before: Put everything in the slow cooker except the sweetener. Cook on low for 7 to 9 hours.

In the morning: Stir the mixture to get a consistent texture, add your sweetener, and stir again.

YIELD: about 3 cups (700 g)
PER 1-CUP (233 G) SERVING: 163.3 calories; 4.0 g total fat; 0.3 g saturated fat; 5.3 g protein; 20.0 g carbohydrate; 3.3 g dietary fiber; 0 mg cholesterol
PREP TIME: 5 minutes
COOKING TIME: 7 to 9 hours

INDIAN CARROT HALWA OATMEAL

★ SOY-FREE   ★ GLUTEN-FREE   ★ OIL-FREE OPTION*

Carrot halwa is an Indian dessert that's a thick paste of carrot, sugar, and cardamom.
It's sometimes topped with saffron and pistachios. If you're not sure whether you're a fan
of cardamom, just use ½ teaspoon instead of a whole teaspoon.
You can always add more before serving.

½ cup (40 g) steel-cut oats

2 cups (475 ml) unsweetened
nondairy milk

1 cup (110 g) grated carrots

1 teaspoon ground cardamom

Sweetener of your choice, to taste
(I use ¼ teaspoon stevia.)

For serving: pinch saffron and
4 teaspoons (12 g) chopped
pistachios

The night before: Spray your crock with oil to help with cleanup later
or skip it* and just plan on soaking your crock immediately afterward
so any stuck-on oatmeal will come right off.

Add oats, nondairy milk, carrots, and cardamom. Cook on low
overnight, 7 to 9 hours.

In the morning: Stir your oatmeal well. It may seem watery at the top,
but if stirred, it should attain a more uniform consistency.

Stir in the sweetener and the saffron if you're using it. Top each
serving with 1 teaspoon of pistachios.

YIELD: about 4 cups (932 g)
PER 1-CUP (233 G) SERVING: 135.0 calories; 4.1 g total fat; 0.3 g saturated fat;
5.0 g protein; 22.8 g carbohydrate; 4.4 g dietary fiber; 0 mg cholesterol
PREP TIME: 10 minutes
COOKING TIME: 7 to 9 hours

DID YOU KNOW?
Saffron is so expensive because it's the stigma of a flower and
needs to be harvested by hand one strand at a time. If you grow
calendula (also called pot marigold), you can dry the leaves to use
in place of saffron. It provides great color, but only real saffron has
that great taste and aroma.

CHAPTER FOUR

DIP DINNERS:
APPETIZERS OR A MEAL

I LOVE HAVING APPETIZERS FOR A MEAL. It just seems so indulgent, and I feel a little bit like I'm going against the rules. Creamy fondues, slow-cooker veggie toppings on bruschetta, even warm tomato cheezy dips for your favorite bread sticks all make a fun and easy dinner at the end of a long day.

   These are great choices for parties because as appetizers they can serve more. And your guests will probably request that you bring them to their next dinner!

EGGPLANT TAPENADE

★ SOY-FREE   ★ GLUTEN-FREE   ★ OIL-FREE

The slow cooker is eggplant's best friend. This warm veggie spread will prove it to you.
Plus you can make it chunky or smooth—it's your call.

3 cups (246 g) chopped eggplant

1½ cups (270 g) diced tomatoes or 1 can (14.5 ounces, or 410 g) undrained

1 can (6 ounces, or 170 g) pitted green olives, chopped

4 cloves garlic, minced

2 teaspoons (5.7 g) capers

1 to 2 teaspoons (5 to 10 ml) balsamic vinegar

1 teaspoon dried or 1 tablespoon (2.5 g) fresh basil

Salt and pepper, to taste

Add everything above balsamic vinegar to the slow cooker and cook on low for 7 to 9 hours.

Before serving add the vinegar, basil, salt, and pepper. Taste and adjust seasonings as needed.

You can either leave it chunky for bruschetta or purée it in a food processor until you have tiny pieces for crackers or crostini.

YIELD: about 4 cups (720 g)

PER 2-TABLESPOON (22 G) SERVING: 12.2 calories; 0.9 g total fat; 0.1 g saturated fat; 0.2 g protein; 1.2 g carbohydrate; 0.5 g dietary fiber; 0 mg cholesterol

PREP TIME: 15 minutes

COOKING TIME: 7 to 9 hours

RECIPE VARIATION
I love this veggie combo, but if you aren't in love with olives, just leave them out.

ALMOND AND GREAT NORTHERN BEAN FONDUE

★ SOY-FREE OPTION*   ★ GLUTEN-FREE OPTION**   ★ OIL-FREE

This deceptively simple dip fits in the grooviest '70s fondue party and works
just as well as a weeknight meal. You can serve it with steamed veggies, toasted bread cubes
(use gluten-free), or tempeh. Another great way to dress it up is to mix in some green
or puréed veggies, which you can vary each time you make it.

FOR THE MORNING INGREDIENTS:

1¼ cups (285 ml) water

½ cup (55 g) slivered almonds

¼ cup (48 g) dried great northern beans

FOR THE EVENING INGREDIENTS:

1 teaspoon nutritional yeast flakes

¼ teaspoon salt

¼ teaspoon pepper

FOR THE DIPPERS:

Toasted bread cubes (**use gluten-free)

Steamed baby carrots

Steamed broccoli

Seared pressed tofu cubes (*omit if soy-free)

Steamed tempeh (*omit if soy-free)

In the morning: Add the morning ingredients to your slow cooker and cook on low for 7 to 9 hours.

Before serving: Carefully pour the contents of the slow cooker into your blender. Add the evening ingredients and purée until smooth.

You can pour the mixture back into the slow cooker and turn to warm. That way you can dip your goodies right into the slow cooker.

YIELD: about 3 cups (738 g)

PER 2-TABLESPOON (31 G) SERVING (WITHOUT DIPPERS): 19.9 calories; 1.2 g total fat; 0.1 g saturated fat; 1.0 g protein; 1.7 g carbohydrate; 0.7 g dietary fiber; 0 mg cholesterol

PREP TIME: 10 minutes

COOKING TIME: 7 to 9 hours

DID YOU KNOW?

Fondue parties are fun to throw. Add in a little Tom Jones, some thrift store dresses, rosé wine, and no one will ever forget it. My best one even included a tacky electric fireplace!

SIMPLE RED PEPPER
GARLIC BEAN DIP

★ SOY-FREE   ★ GLUTEN-FREE   ★ OIL-FREE

This super-easy, protein-rich bean dip is so versatile. You can use any dry beans
(except kidney beans) that you have in your pantry or throw in a mix of different beans.

1 cup (235 ml) water

½ cup (112 g) dried beans, such
as pinto, black, vaquero, etc.

10 cloves garlic

1 cup (150 g) red pepper, chopped

Salt and pepper, to taste

Add all the ingredients except for the salt and pepper to your slow
cooker and cook on low for 7 to 9 hours.

Once cooked, drain the beans into a measuring cup or bowl and
reserve the liquid. Put the bean mixture in a food processor and process
until smooth, adding some of the cooking liquid as needed to make it
the thickness you prefer. Discard any leftover liquid.

YIELD: about 3 cups (738 g)
PER 2-TABLESPOON (31 G) SERVING: 17.7 calories; 0.1 g total fat; 0 g saturated
fat; 1.1 g protein; 3.4 g carbohydrate; 1.1 g dietary fiber; 0 mg cholesterol
PREP TIME: 10 minutes
COOKING TIME: 7 to 9 hours

RECIPE VARIATION
Add a little Mexican flavor by adding ½ teaspoon of cumin and a little
chili pepper. You could also use white beans and throw in some fresh
basil in the food processor for another variation. This is a great base
to play with your favorite beans and seasonings.

EASIER-THAN-PIZZA DIP

★ SOY-FREE   ★ GLUTEN-FREE OPTION*   ★ OIL-FREE

I love bread sticks, and this is the ultimate dipping sauce for them.
You can customize it with your favorites including chopped vegan pepperoni,
minced Italian Seitan Coins (page 16, *omit if gluten-free), chopped olives, and more!

FOR THE DIP BASE:

1 can (14.5 ounces, or 411 g) crushed or puréed tomatoes

¼ cup Nut Ricotta (page 25)

¼ cup (30 g) bell pepper, minced

1 tablespoon (5.5 g) cooked onion (page 19)

1 clove garlic, minced

½ teaspoon balsamic vinegar

½ teaspoon dried oregano

½ teaspoon dried basil

Salt and pepper, to taste

EXTRAS:

Chopped vegan pepperoni (*omit if gluten-free)

Minced Italian Seitan Coins (page 16, *omit if gluten-free)

Make-Your-Own Gluten Crumbles (recipe page 10, *omit if gluten-free) or store-bought

Chopped mushrooms

Chopped olives

Minced sun-dried tomatoes

Add everything in the dip base list except the salt and pepper. Cook on high for 1 to 1½ hours. Add salt and pepper to taste, add the extras to customize, and cook another 30 minutes or until the dip is piping hot.

Serving suggestions: Serve with bread sticks (*use gluten-free), focaccia wedges (*use gluten-free), or even lightly steamed veggies. You can also call it a fondue and serve at a fancy cocktail party.

YIELD: about 3 cups (735 g)
PER 2-TABLESPOON (30 G) SERVING (NOT INCLUDING EXTRAS): 143 calories; 11.8 g total fat; 1.8 g saturated fat; 4.0 g protein; 8 g carbohydrate; 1.6 g dietary fiber; 0 mg cholesterol
PREP TIME: 10 minutes
COOKING TIME: 1½ to 2 hours

MIX-AND-MATCH SOUTHWEST FONDUE

★ SOY-FREE   ★ GLUTEN-FREE OPTION*   ★ OIL-FREE

This is one of my all-time favorite dip dinners. I've always been partial to nachos,
and this dip is less work than they are and tastes even better. You can make it healthier
by dipping steamed whole-wheat tortillas (*use gluten-free) in it instead of the usual fried chips.

FOR THE MORNING INGREDIENTS:

1½ cups (355 ml) unsweetened nondairy milk

1 cup (140 g) cashews

FOR THE EVENING INGREDIENTS:

1 teaspoon apple cider vinegar

1 teaspoon chili powder

2 cloves minced garlic or ½ teaspoon granulated garlic

¼ to ½ teaspoon salt, to taste

EXTRAS:

1½ cups (258 g) cooked black beans (or 1 can [14.5 ounces, or 410 g], rinsed)

1 cup (180 g) diced tomatoes

2 tablespoons (18 g) green chiles

1 teaspoon minced jalapeños, optional

Steamed whole-wheat tortillas, for dipping (*use gluten-free)

Steamed veggies, for dipping

Baked tortilla chips, for dipping

In the morning: Add the morning ingredients to your slow cooker and cook on low for 7 to 9 hours.

Thirty minutes before serving: Carefully transfer the cooked mixture to your blender, add the evening ingredients, and blend until smooth and creamy.

Pour back into the slow cooker. Add any extras, turn the slow cooker to high, and cook for 30 to 45 minutes until the dip is piping hot.

YIELD: about 3 cups (700 ml)

PER 2-TABLESPOON (28 ML) SERVING (WITHOUT EXTRAS): 56.8 calories; 4.6 g total fat; 0 g saturated fat; 0.1 g protein; 2.8 g carbohydrate; 0.4 g dietary fiber; 0 mg cholesterol

PREP TIME: 15 minutes

COOKING TIME: 7½ to 10 hours

DID YOU KNOW?

Most cans that contain cooked beans are lined with the compound BPA (Bisphenol A). Health safety concerns have been raised about the effect of BPA on the endocrine system. Some companies are switching to other linings or even non-can packaging, but you can easily avoid canned beans and make your own for less money—and more peace of mind—using the Small Batch Dry Beans recipe (page 24).

CAN'T-BE-BEAT CURRIED BEAN DIP

★ SOY-FREE   ★ GLUTEN-FREE   ★ OIL-FREE

This is great as a dip or even as a sandwich spread on a tortilla or some roti bread.
If you're near an Indian store, grab some pappadums to use as dippers. The dip's heat
depends on how you make your sambar powder, but feel free to add an extra
ground chile pepper if you want to stoke up the flames!

1½ cups (355 ml) water

¼ cup (48 g) red lentils

¼ cup (48 g) moong dal (golden lentils)

1½ teaspoons (4 g) grated ginger

1 teaspoon Garam Masala (page 21)

½ teaspoon Sambar Spice Powder (page 21), optional

2 cloves garlic, minced

Salt, to taste

1 tablespoon (1 g) minced fresh cilantro, optional

Add everything except for the salt and cilantro to your slow cooker.
Cook on low for 7 to 9 hours.

Before serving, add salt to suit your taste and cilantro (if using).

YIELD: about 3 cups (738 g)
PER 2-TABLESPOON (31 G) SERVING: 10 calories; 0 g total fat; 0 g saturated
fat; 0.8 g protein; 1.8 g carbohydrate; 0.7 g dietary fiber; 0 mg cholesterol
PREP TIME: 10 minutes
COOKING TIME: 7 to 9 hours

RECIPE VARIATION
Mix in some minced greens in the last 20 minutes of cooking to add
color and extra vitamins.

—CHAPTER FIVE—

SOUL SATISFIERS:
SOUPS FOR ALL SEASONS

SLOW COOKERS REALLY EXCEL AT MAKING SOUPS. If you're not sure just how long you'll be at work, one of these soups can save the day. They can cook a few hours longer because they already contain lots of liquid—there's no need to worry your meal will turn out overcooked or dry.

One of the best things about soup as a meal is that the variety is staggering—you can enjoy Every Season Minestrone (page 61) on Monday, Creamy Green Chile Corn Chowder (page 73) on Tuesday, Indian Sambar (page 64) on Wednesday, Moroccan Lentil Vegetable Soup (page 70) on Thursday, and a cashew-based Creamy Tomato Basil Bisque (page 75) to start the weekend off right.

And many of your favorite soups, traditionally prepared over the stovetop, can be made in the slow cooker. If they're creamy, just add nondairy milks at the end of cooking time with any short-cooking vegetables.

There's not much that's more soothing than coming home to a piping hot bowl of homemade soup, especially when it's this easy.

EVERY SEASON MINESTRONE

★ SOY-FREE ★ GLUTEN-FREE OPTION* ★ OIL-FREE OPTION**

Minestrone is a delightful Italian veggie soup. It's also easily adapted so you can use what's in your CSA box or garden. Feel free to adapt to include your favorite veggies.

FOR THE MORNING INGREDIENTS:

2 cups (475 ml) water

¾ cup (135 g) diced tomatoes

¾ cup (134 g) cooked white beans

½ cup (60 g) summer or (70 g) winter squash, diced

¼ cup (25 g) diced celery or (39 g) celeriac

¼ cup (33 g) carrots or sweet potato, diced

1 vegan bouillon cube

2 cloves garlic, minced

1 tablespoon (5.5 g) cooked onion (page 19)

½ teaspoon dried oregano

½ teaspoon dried marjoram

¼ teaspoon ground rosemary or ½ teaspoon fresh rosemary

FOR THE EVENING INGREDIENTS:

½ cup (50 g) chopped green beans or greens

EXTRAS:

Cooked small pasta shapes such as stars or tiny shells (*use gluten-free)

Chopped fresh basil

Vegan Parmesan (**omit if oil-free)

In the morning: Add all the morning ingredients to the slow cooker and cook on low for 7 to 9 hours.

Thirty minutes before serving: Add green beans or greens (or even a combination of the two) to the slow cooker and turn to high. The soup is finished once these veggies are cooked through, about 30 minutes.

Serve topped with chopped fresh basil, a ladle full of pasta, and a little sprinkle of vegan Parmesan (**omit if oil-free) to make this an amazing one-bowl meal.

YIELD: about 3 cups (700 ml)
PER 1-CUP (235 ML) SERVING (WITHOUT PASTA): 142.2 calories; 2.2 g total fat; 0.1 g saturated fat; 6.4 g protein; 26.7 g carbohydrate; 6.3 g dietary fiber; 0 mg cholesterol
PREP TIME: 5 minutes
COOKING TIME: 7½ to 9½ hours

DID YOU KNOW?
Celeriac, or celery root, is not the root of the celery plant we buy in the store. Instead, it's a different variety that doesn't produce large stalks of celery.

OLD-FASHIONED TOMATO VEGETABLE SOUP

★ SOY-FREE   ★ GLUTEN-FREE   ★ OIL-FREE

Sometimes, you need a little nostalgia in your bowl. This soup is perfect after a day playing in the snow or even after a long day at work. Adding turnips and cabbage makes it heartier than the veggie soup you probably grew up on. If you're afraid of that turnip tanginess, don't worry, they mellow out, and you'll barely know they are there.

1½ cups (270 g) diced tomatoes

1 cup (235 ml) water

¾ cup (75 g) green beans, broken into ½-inch (1.3 cm) pieces

½ cup (55 g) diced potatoes

½ cup (75 g) diced turnip

½ cup (45 g) chopped cabbage

2 tablespoons (11 g) cooked onion (page 19)

2 tablespoons (19 g) diced green pepper

1 vegan bouillon cube

Salt and pepper, to taste

Add everything except for the salt and pepper to the slow cooker and cook on low for 7 to 9 hours.

Before serving, thin with water if the soup is too thick. Add salt and pepper.

YIELD: about 4 cups (950 ml)
PER 1-CUP (235 ML) SERVING: 63.5 CALORIES; 2.8 g total fat; 0 g saturated fat; 1.8 g protein; 9.6 g carbohydrate; 2.4 g dietary fiber; 0 mg cholesterol
PREP TIME: 5 minutes
COOKING TIME: 7 to 9 hours

RECIPE VARIATION
Make some grilled (vegan) cheez sandwiches and mugs of hot chocolate to complete a perfect winter scene.

CREAMY CELERY ROOT SOUP

★ SOY-FREE   ★ GLUTEN-FREE   ★ OIL-FREE

Celery root, also known as celeriac, is one of my favorite veggies.
It's also one of the ugliest, but don't let that put you off it. Once you peel it,
there is a light green creamy root with a subtle flavor of celery.

3 cups (312 g) celery root, peeled and chopped

2 cups (475 ml) water

⅓ cup (47 g) cashews

¼ cup (22 g) chopped leeks or 2 tablespoons (11 g) cooked onion (page 19)

1 vegan bouillon cube

1 teaspoon dried thyme

Salt and pepper, to taste

Add everything except salt and pepper to the slow cooker and cook on low for 7 to 9 hours.

Purée the soup in a blender. Taste and add salt and pepper.

YIELD: about 5 cups (1.2 L)

PER 1-CUP (235 ML) SERVING: 94.1 calories; 4.3 g total fat; 0 g saturated fat; 0.1 g protein; 3.1 g carbohydrate; 0.4 g dietary fiber; 0 mg cholesterol

PREP TIME: 15 minutes

COOKING TIME: 7 to 9 hours

DID YOU KNOW?
Celery root is full of vitamin K, vitamin C, and fiber. You lose some of the celery root as you trim its tentacled root offshoots and peel the thick skin. Rinse off after you trim it up as dirt can hide in its intricate nooks and crannies.

INDIAN SAMBAR

★ SOY-FREE   ★ GLUTEN-FREE   ★ OIL-FREE

Sambar is a versatile bowl of lentils and seasonal veggies. It has a slightly tart and tangy flavor from the tamarind paste. The aroma is heavenly because of the sambar spice powder, which contains ground lentils, coriander, mustard seeds, cumin, and fenugreek. It's usually eaten at any time of the day with dosas, an Indian crepe typically filled with spiced potatoes, but it's great all by itself, too. Plus, you can vary the veggies depending on what you have in your fridge.

2½ cups (570 ml) water

⅓ cup (64 g) uncooked toor or moong dal (or other split yellow lentil)

1 tablespoon (11 g) Sambar Spice Powder (page 21)

1 small carrot, diced

1 medium potato, diced

1 tablespoon (5.5 g) cooked onion (page 19)

1 teaspoon turmeric

1 teaspoon tamarind paste

½ teaspoon (1 to 2) curry leaves, optional

Salt, to taste

Add everything except the salt to the slow cooker and cook on low for 7 to 9 hours.

Stir, add salt, taste, and adjust any seasonings as needed.

YIELD: about 3 cups (700 ml)
PER 1-CUP (235 ML) SERVING: 100.4 calories; 2.5 g total fat; 0.1 g saturated fat; 3.2 g protein; 18.5 g carbohydrate; 3.6 g dietary fiber; 0 mg cholesterol
PREP TIME: 5 minutes
COOKING TIME: 7 to 9 hours

RECIPE VARIATIONS

- When my friend Kalpana had her restaurant, she would make different sambar variations almost every day. Try adding winter squash, summer squash, greens, or whatever you have ready in the garden. Just add longer-cooking veggies such as roots or winter squash in the beginning. For greens and other quicker-cooking veggies, add 30 minutes before serving and turn to high.
- Add more water after cooking if you like a thinner consistency.

WHITE BEAN QUINOA GUMBO

★ SOY-FREE ★ GLUTEN-FREE ★ OIL-FREE

This is a wholesome twist to the traditional Louisiana okra stew. This one adds nutrition-packed quinoa in place of the usual rice. Serve with your favorite hot sauce on the side.

FOR THE MORNING INGREDIENTS:

2½ cups (570 ml) water

1 cup (100 g) sliced okra

¼ cup (48 g) dry Great Northern beans or other small white bean

1 tablespoon (5.5 g) cooked onion (page 19), minced

2 tablespoons (15 g) celery, minced

2 cloves garlic, minced

1 vegan bouillon cube

2 bay leaves

½ teaspoon dried oregano

¼ to ½ teaspoon cayenne pepper, to taste

2 whole allspice berries

FOR THE EVENING INGREDIENTS:

1 cup (180 g) diced tomatoes

⅛ cup (22 g) quinoa

1 teaspoon dried oregano

¼ teaspoon chili powder

¼ teaspoon ground cumin

Salt and pepper

In the morning: Add all the morning ingredients and cook on low for 7 to 9 hours.

Thirty minutes before serving: Add all the evening ingredients except the salt and pepper. Mix well. Cook for 30 minutes on low.

Before serving, add salt and pepper. Taste and adjust any of the seasonings as needed. Remove allspice berries and bay leaves before serving.

YIELD: about 5 cups (1.2 L)

PER 1-CUP (235 ML) SERVING: 89.7 calories; 1.6 g total fat; 0 g saturated fat; 4.6 g protein; 15.5 g carbohydrate; 3.5 g dietary fiber; 0 mg cholesterol

PREP TIME: 10 minutes

COOKING TIME: 7½ to 9½ hours

RECIPE VARIATIONS

- Use small red beans or even chickpeas in place of the white beans if you don't have any on hand.
- Feel free to add any seasonal veggies you have on hand. This is a perfect stew to help you clean out the fridge!

WHITE BEAN DELICATA SOUP

★ SOY-FREE   ★ GLUTEN-FREE   ★ OIL-FREE

This simple soup goes great with a green salad full of slices of fresh, ripe pear.
No delicata? Feel free to substitute any winter squash. I talked my friend Christy
into trying her first delicata, and now this is her favorite soup!

2½ cups (570 ml) water

2 cups (280 g) delicata squash,
peeled and diced

½ cup (96 g) dry (uncooked) white
beans

2 vegan bouillon cubes

Four 2-inch (5 cm) sprigs fresh
thyme or 1 teaspoon dried thyme

One 2-inch (5 cm) sprig fresh
rosemary or ½ teaspoon dried
rosemary

Smoked salt and pepper, to taste

Add everything except salt and pepper to the slow cooker and cook on
low for 7 to 9 hours.

Remove the thyme and rosemary stems. Taste and add salt and
pepper.

YIELD: about 5 cups (1.2 L)
PER 1-CUP (235 ML) SERVING: 108 calories; 0.2 g total fat; 0.1 g saturated fat;
6.2 g protein; 21.0 g carbohydrate; 5.4 g dietary fiber; 0 mg cholesterol
PREP TIME: 5 minutes
COOKING TIME: 7 to 9 hours

DID YOU KNOW?
There are dozens of varieties of beans that are white, and most
are interchangeable depending on what you have on hand. Great
Northern beans or navy beans are easy to find, but if you're feeling
adventurous, go to ranchogordo.com and explore the heirloom
varieties, some of which you may not know exist.

CURRIED EGGPLANT AND PEPPER SOUP

★ SOY-FREE   ★ GLUTEN-FREE   ★ OIL-FREE

If you are looking for a light soup to go with your kale salad, this is the one for you. It's a thinner soup that has a hint of curry mixed in with the earthiness of the eggplant. I like mine puréed, but leave it chunky if that makes you happy!

2 cups (475 g) water

2 cups (164 g) eggplant, chopped

1 cup (150 g) bell pepper, chopped

2 tablespoons (11 g) cooked onion (page 19), minced

½ teaspoon Garam Masala (recipe on page 21 or a store-bought mix)

½ teaspoon chili powder, or to taste

Salt and pepper, to taste

Add everything except salt and pepper to the slow cooker and cook on low for 7 to 9 hours.

Purée the soup in a blender or with an immersion blender (or you can leave it chunky). Taste and add salt and pepper. Add more garam masala and/or chili powder if needed.

YIELD: about 5 cups (1.2 L)
PER 1-CUP (235 ML) SERVING: 27.1 calories; 2.3 g total fat; 0 g saturated fat; 0.5 g protein; 3.4 g carbohydrate; 1.5 g dietary fiber; 0 mg cholesterol
PREP TIME: 10 minutes
COOKING TIME: 7 to 9 hours

RECIPE VARIATION
Try this with cauliflower or potato in place of the eggplant for a winter variation.

MOROCCAN LENTIL VEGETABLE SOUP

★ SOY-FREE   ★ GLUTEN-FREE   ★ OIL-FREE

This is a filling bowl of nutritious veggie soup made hearty with red lentils. But it's the spices that make it stand out. Sumac has a sour taste similar to lemon, and the cinnamon adds that touch of sweetness that's so wonderful in Moroccan cuisine. Feel free to switch up the veggies with the seasons.

2 cups (475 g) water

½ cup (96 g) red lentils

½ cup (60 g) chopped zucchini

½ cup (60 g) chopped yellow squash

¼ cup (33 g) carrot, cut into half moons

¼ cup (45 g) minced tomatoes

⅛ cup (19 g) bell pepper, minced

2 cloves garlic, minced

½ teaspoon dried oregano

¼ teaspoon ground cumin

¼ teaspoon smoked paprika

¼ teaspoon ground cinnamon

¼ teaspoon ground sumac, optional

Salt and pepper, to taste

Add everything except for the sumac, if using, salt, and pepper to the slow cooker. Cook on low for 7 to 9 hours.

When done, add sumac, salt, and pepper. Taste and adjust seasonings as needed.

YIELD: about 4 cups (950 ml)

PER 1-CUP (235 ML) SERVING: 98.6 calories; 0.3 g total fat; 0.1 g saturated fat; 6.6 g protein; 17.9 g carbohydrate; 3.8 g dietary fiber; 0 mg cholesterol

PREP TIME: 15 minutes

COOKING TIME: 7 to 9 hours

DID YOU KNOW?

Sumac is a little tart and can be used wherever you might add a squeeze of lemon. Sumac is actually a dried, ground berry from a shrub that has no relation to poison sumac. You can find it online, at specialty spice stores, or in Middle Eastern markets.

CREAMY GREEN CHILE CORN CHOWDER

★ SOY-FREE OPTION* ★ GLUTEN-FREE OPTION** ★ OIL-FREE OPTION***

This is a great light summer soup when fresh corn is in season. All you need is a big green salad to complete your meal. The addition of corncobs to flavor the broth really gives it a rich and cohesive feel.

1½ cups (231 g) fresh corn kernels (about 3 small ears)

1 or 2 corncobs to flavor the broth

One 3-inch (7.5 cm) piece carrot

2 cups (475 g) water

1 tablespoon (5.5 g) cooked onion (page 19), minced

1 tablespoon (7.5 g) green chiles

½ teaspoon chili powder

¼ teaspoon jalapeño powder or jalapeño salt

Vegan sour cream, *Cashew Cream (page 28), or ***Extra-Thick Silken Tofu Sour Cream (page 28) for topping

Add everything except for the optional sour cream to the slow cooker and cook on low for 6 to 9 hours.

Remove the corncobs and then use an immersion blender to purée the mixture (or purée it in a blender). Taste and then add salt and pepper. Adjust the chili powder or jalapeño powder to suit your taste.

Serve topped with a dollop of vegan sour cream, Cashew Cream, or Extra-Thick Silken Tofu Sour Cream.

YIELD: about 4 cups (950 ml)
PER 1-CUP (235 ML) SERVING: 68.8 calories; 3.3 g total fat; 0.3 g saturated fat; 1.8 g protein; 11.5 g carbohydrate; 2.2 g dietary fiber; 0 mg cholesterol
PREP TIME: 15 minutes
COOKING TIME: 6 to 9 hours

RECIPE VARIATION
Make this recipe in the dead of winter by using frozen corn. Just add a veggie bouillon cube to add more flavor to the broth since you won't be using corncobs.

WHITE BEAN BARLEY SOUP

★ SOY-FREE ★ GLUTEN-FREE ★ OIL-FREE

This is the soup to throw together before you leave for work. You'll be glad you did, once you curl up in front of the fireplace and eat it with a crusty piece of bread. It's thick and full of flavor, so it's perfect for a simple one-bowl meal. Sometimes simple meals are the best!

3 cups (700 ml) water

¾ cup (144 g) dry navy or great northern beans

½ cup (35 g) mushrooms (Try adding shiitake or portobello.)

¼ cup (50 g) barley

1 tablespoon (5.5 g) cooked onion (page 19)

1 clove garlic, minced

2 vegan bouillon cubes

One 2-inch (5 cm) sprig fresh rosemary or ½ teaspoon dried rosemary

½ teaspoon dried thyme

¼ teaspoon jalapeño powder or your favorite hot pepper powder

Smoked salt (or regular salt with a few drops of liquid smoke) and pepper, to taste

Add everything except for the salt and pepper to the slow cooker. Cook on low for 7 to 9 hours. Before serving, add smoked salt and pepper to taste.

YIELD: about 3 cups (700 ml)
PER 1-CUP (235 ML) SERVING: 264.3 calories; 2.9 g total fat; 0.1 g saturated fat; 13.3 g protein; 49.2 g carbohydrate; 17.1 g dietary fiber; 0 mg cholesterol
PREP TIME: 5 minutes
COOKING TIME: 7 to 9 hours

DID YOU KNOW?
Jalapeño powder is great to have in your spice cabinet. I love mixing it with a little salt and serving it on top of a big bowl of grits. It takes almost no effort but yields a big flavor. You can order it online if you can't find it in your area.

CREAMY TOMATO BASIL BISQUE

★ SOY-FREE   ★ GLUTEN-FREE   ★ OIL-FREE

This is the vegan version of the thick, rich tomato basil soups you find at restaurants.
It's so simple to make that you can have it whenever you want it. And no one
will guess it's vegan unless you tell them.

FOR THE MORNING INGREDIENTS:

2 cans (14.5 ounces, or 410 g each)
or 3 cups (540 g) diced tomatoes

¼ cup (60 g) water, if using fresh
tomatoes

¼ cup (35 g) cashews

5 whole cloves garlic

2 teaspoons (1.5 g) dried basil

FOR THE EVENING INGREDIENTS:

½ to 1 cup (120 to 235 g)
unsweetened nondairy milk

1 tablespoon (2.5 g) fresh basil,
optional

Salt and pepper, to taste

In the morning: Add all of the morning ingredients to the slow cooker
and cook on low for 7 to 9 hours. Note: If using fresh tomatoes, there
will be less liquid than if you are using canned ones, so you will need
the ¼ cup (60 ml) water to balance things out.

Before serving: Carefully pour the contents of the slow cooker into a
blender. Add ½ cup (120 ml) nondairy milk and fresh basil, if using. Blend
until silky smooth. Add the other ½ cup (120 ml) milk if the soup needs
to be thinner. Add salt and pepper to taste. If you are not using the
optional fresh basil, add more dried basil if needed.

YIELD: about 4 cups (950 ml)
PER 1-CUP (235 ML) SERVING: 96 CALORIES; 4.3 g total fat; 0.3 g saturated fat;
3.4 g protein; 9 g carbohydrate; 2.8 g dietary fiber; 0 mg cholesterol
PREP TIME: 5 minutes
COOKING TIME: 7 to 9 hours

RECIPE VARIATION

Make other rich creamy soups by using the vegetables you have
on hand in place of the tomatoes. If it's a delicate veggie such as
asparagus or broccoli, add it in the last 30 minutes of cooking time
instead of in the beginning.

AUTUMN HARVEST VEGGIE SOUP

★ SOY-FREE   ★ GLUTEN-FREE   ★ OIL-FREE

You can't go wrong with brussels sprouts and winter squash. Put them in a soup together, add sage, thyme, a hint of apple cider vinegar, and you'll be eating a bowl of fall for dinner.

2 cups (475 g) water

1½ cups (210 g) diced winter squash

1 cup (88 g) shredded brussels sprouts

½ cup (65 g) diced carrots

¼ cup (38 g) diced bell pepper

2 tablespoons (11 g) cooked onion (page 19)

1 clove garlic, minced

1 vegan bouillon cube

1 teaspoon dried sage

2 teaspoons (2 g) dried thyme

1 teaspoon apple cider vinegar

Salt and pepper, to taste

Toasted minced pecans for garnish, optional

Add everything except the last three ingredients to the slow cooker and cook on low for 7 to 9 hours.

Before serving, add apple cider vinegar, salt, and pepper. Serve with a sprinkling of toasted pecans.

YIELD: about 5 cups (1.2 L)
PER 1-CUP (235 ML) SERVING: 51.2 calories; 2.3 g total fat; 0 g saturated fat; 1.3 g protein; 9.4 g carbohydrate; 2.9 g dietary fiber; 0 mg cholesterol
PREP TIME: 20 minutes
COOKING TIME: 7 to 9 hours

RECIPE VARIATION
This soup just begs to be made for your Thanksgiving celebration. You can even use pumpkin instead of winter squash.

CURRIED CIDER WINTER SQUASH SOUP

★ SOY-FREE   ★ GLUTEN-FREE   ★ OIL-FREE

This soup is reminiscent of colorful fall leaves and perfect for Thanksgiving dinner. I originally used a special fall hard cider that already had some cinnamon and nutmeg in it, but you can use plain hard cider and add the spices yourself to make it any time.

2 cups (280 g) diced winter squash

1 bottle (12 ounces, or 355 ml) hard cider

2 cloves garlic, minced

1 teaspoon Garam Masala (page 21)

½ teaspoon ground cinnamon

¼ teaspoon ground nutmeg

½ cup (120 ml) unsweetened nondairy milk

Salt and pepper, to taste

Add everything except for the nondairy milk, salt, and pepper to the slow cooker. Cook on low for 7 to 9 hours.

Carefully add the cooked mixture to a blender. Add the nondairy milk, salt, and pepper. Purée and then taste and adjust any of the spices as needed.

YIELD: about 3 cups (700 ml)
PER 1-CUP (235 ML) SERVING: 154.3 calories; 0.7 g total fat; 0 g saturated fat; 1.9 g protein; 308 g carbohydrate; 6.2 g dietary fiber; 0 mg cholesterol
PREP TIME: 15 minutes
COOKING TIME: 7 to 9 hours

RECIPE VARIATION
If you aren't a fan of curry, leave out the garam masala and add a pinch or two of cinnamon and a little allspice instead.

CHAPTER SIX

INTERNATIONAL EATS:
STEWS, CURRIES, AND CHILI

STEWS ARE SOME OF MY FAVORITE MEALS. They have long cooking times, so they are perfect for people who work away from home. If you think you'll be away longer than 9 hours, just add some extra liquid, and you'll be all set.

If that's not enough incentive, take a look at the recipe list below. Kiss expensive takeout good-bye and make your own exotic meals at home. I promise you won't miss them at all once you have these delicious stews and curries. (And think of the vacation you can take with all the money you'll save!)

UNSTUFFED POTATOES

★ GLUTEN-FREE   ★ SOY-FREE OPTION*   ★ OIL-FREE OPTION**

I love baked potatoes, and they are perfect as a main course. These unstuffed potatoes have all the great ingredients and flavors with much less work. A bowl of these creamy, cheezy potatoes is reminiscent of a traditional stuffed baked potato. It's easier to eat, though, and you get a little bit of everything in each creamy bite.

FOR THE MORNING INGREDIENTS:

2 medium baking potatoes (skin on if using organic), chopped

1½ cups (355 ml) water

FOR THE EVENING INGREDIENTS:

¼ cup (60 g) vegan sour cream, *Cashew Cream (page 28), **or Extra-Thick Silken Tofu Sour Cream (page 28)

2 tablespoons (12 g) nutritional yeast flakes

1 tablespoon (14 g) vegan butter or olive oil (**omit for oil-free)

1 tablespoon (3 g) fresh chives, minced, optional

Smoked salt and pepper, to taste

EXTRAS:

Shredded vegan cheese (**omit for oil-free)

Tempeh bacon crumbles (*omit for soy-free)

Extra chopped chives

Steamed veggies

In the morning: Add the potatoes and water to the slow cooker. Cook on low for 7 to 9 hours.

In the evening: Using pot holders, remove the crock. Then carefully pour the water out of the crock into a measuring cup and set aside.

Fold in the evening ingredients gently, so you don't end up with mashed potatoes. Add about 2 tablespoons (28 ml) of the water that you drained off earlier.

Serve topped with any extras you'd like.

YIELD: about 4 cups (900 g)

PER 1-CUP (225 G) SERVING (WITHOUT EXTRAS): 152.1 calories; 6.2 g total fat; 1 g saturated fat; 4.3 g protein; 21.9 g carbohydrate; 4.3 g dietary fiber; 0 mg cholesterol

PREP TIME: 10 minutes

COOKING TIME: 7 to 9 hours

RECIPE VARIATION

Serve over fresh spinach. The heat of the potato mixture will slightly cook the spinach, and it will be beautiful, too!

ITALIAN SEITAN AND PEPPER STEW

★ SOY-FREE   ★ OIL-FREE

This simple dish goes great over rice or pasta as well as stuffed in a crusty baguette
for an Italian sausage sandwich. No matter how you serve it, everyone will love it. The aroma
of the Italian seasonings with the peppers and onions reminds me of Italian street fare.
The Italian Seitan Coins make it a hearty meal, but you can use store-bought seitan
or vegan Italian sausage if you don't have the coins already made.

¾ cup (175 ml) Italian Seitan Coins
(page 16)

1½ cups (270 g) diced tomatoes

½ cup (44 g) cooked onion
(page 19)

½ cup (75 g) chopped bell pepper

½ cup (120 ml) water or vegetable
broth

1 teaspoon Italian Seasoning
(page 22)

Salt and pepper, to taste

Add everything except the salt and pepper to the slow cooker and cook
on low for 7 to 10 hours.

Stir in salt and pepper, taste, and adjust spices as needed.

YIELD: about 4 cups (772 g)
PER 1-CUP (193 G) SERVING: 86.5 calories; 11 g total fat; 0 g saturated fat;
0.9 g protein; 5.6 g carbohydrate; 1.7 g dietary fiber; 0 mg cholesterol
PREP TIME: 10 minutes
COOKING TIME: 7 to 10 hours

RECIPE VARIATION
This dish is good by itself but even better when served over whole-
wheat pasta. It's perfect for date night.

TOFU AND GRAPE STEW

★ OIL-FREE   ★ SOY-FREE OPTION*   ★ GLUTEN-FREE OPTION**

Are you getting bored with the same old thing? Then this recipe is for you. This is a light, slightly sweet stew that's perfect for a late summer meal. If you avoid soy, substitute seitan or even chickpeas for the tofu.

1½ cups (372 g) tofu, cubed (*use the same amount seitan or chickpeas)

1 cup (150 g) quartered seedless grapes

½ cup (65 g) thinly sliced carrots

¼ cup (60 ml) red wine

¼ cup (60 ml) water

1 bouillon cube

1 teaspoon dried tarragon

¼ cup (15 g) minced fresh parsley

Salt and pepper, to taste

1 to 2 cups (157 to 314 g) cooked whole-wheat couscous (**use brown rice couscous)

Add all the ingredients above the parsley to your slow cooker. Cook on low for 7 to 9 hours.

Before serving, mix in the fresh parsley. Add salt and pepper to taste. Taste and add more tarragon if needed. Serve over couscous.

YIELD: about 4 cups (772 g)

PER 1-CUP (193 G) SERVING (WITHOUT COUSCOUS): 113.6 calories; 8.4 g total fat; 1.3 g saturated fat; 15.4 g protein; 11.2 g carbohydrate; 3.2 g dietary fiber; 0 mg cholesterol

PREP TIME: 15 minutes

COOKING TIME: 7 to 9 hours

DID YOU KNOW?
Couscous is often mistaken for a grain, but it's actually teeny, tiny pasta.

ITALIAN SOY CURLS (WITH BEAN ALTERNATIVE)

★ GLUTEN-FREE OPTION*   ★ OIL-FREE

Since the first time I tasted soy curls I've been hooked. They come dried, but once they are reconstituted, they have a meaty consistency and make any dish heartier. This time they are in a light tomato herb sauce that's great over pasta (*use gluten-free) or as a topping on a vegan pizza.

3 cups (700 ml) puréed tomatoes (fresh or canned)

1 cup (40 g) dry soy curls

1 teaspoon dried basil

½ to 1 teaspoon agave nectar, to taste

½ teaspoon dried oregano

¼ teaspoon dried thyme

⅛ teaspoon ground rosemary or ¼ teaspoon fresh rosemary

Fresh chopped basil, for topping

Salt and pepper, to taste

4 to 6 cups (560 to 840 g) cooked pasta, for serving (*use gluten-free)

Add everything except the fresh basil, salt, and pepper to the slow cooker. Cook on low for 7 to 9 hours.

Add salt and pepper as well as any herb that needs to be a little bolder. Serve over cooked pasta and top with fresh basil.

YIELD: about 4 cups (772 g)
PER 1-CUP (193 G) SERVING (WITHOUT PASTA): 109.5 calories; 1.9 g total fat; 0.2 g saturated fat; 6.4 g protein; 19.8 g carbohydrate; 4.6 g dietary fiber; 0 mg cholesterol
PREP TIME: 15 minutes
COOKING TIME: 7 to 9 hours

RECIPE VARIATIONS
- Top a premade pizza crust with the soy curl mixture and shredded vegan cheese. After you bake it, top with fresh basil. It's delicious!
- Allergic to soy? Substitute 1½ cups (150 g) of cooked beans to bulk up the sauce.

DID YOU KNOW?
Soy curls are simply smashed and dried whole soybeans. No other ingredients or weird processing are involved. In addition, they're not genetically modified. So if you eat soy at all, check them out. You can order them online if you can't get them at a store near you.

GREEN BEANS IN BLACK BEAN SAUCE WITH TOFU

★ OIL-FREE OPTION*

I love the salty-sour taste of fermented black bean paste. It used to be that you could only get it in an Asian market, but now it's in most national grocery chains. Look for it in the international food aisle. This flavorful paste works beautifully in this recipe, which cooks up in about an hour. That makes it perfect for a weekend lunch or dinner.

3 cups (300 g) green beans in ½-inch (1.3 cm) pieces (fresh or frozen)

¼ cup (60 ml) water

7.5 ounces (about 220 g or ½ package) firm tofu, pressed and cut into tiny cubes

2 tablespoons (30 g) black bean paste

1 tablespoon (15 ml) rice wine vinegar or white vinegar

2 teaspoons (10 ml) sesame oil (*omit for oil-free)

¼ to ½ teaspoon chili garlic paste or Sriracha, to taste

1½ to 3 cups (293 to 585 g) cooked brown rice, for serving

Add the green beans and water to the slow cooker. Cook on high for 30 minutes.

While the beans are cooking, mix together the tofu, black bean paste, vinegar, sesame oil, and chili garlic paste or Sriracha and mix well.

After the beans have cooked for 30 minutes, add the tofu mixture and cook until the mixture is hot and the green beans are tender, about 30 minutes to 1 hour more.

Serve over cooked brown rice.

YIELD: about 3 cups (580 g)
PER 1-CUP (193 G) SERVING (WITHOUT BROWN RICE): 169.1 calories; 14.6 g total fat; 2 g saturated fat; 10.5 g protein; 11.5 g carbohydrate; 5 g dietary fiber; 0 mg cholesterol
PREP TIME: 15 minutes
COOKING TIME: 1 to 1½ hours

RECIPE VARIATION
If you can't find black bean paste, try Chinese garlic sauce instead. It's not the same, but it's just as tasty with the combination of tofu and green beans. Don't forget that you can buy black bean paste and chili garlic paste online.

POTATO, GREENS, AND SOY CURL (OR CHICKPEA) CURRY

★ GLUTEN-FREE ★ OIL-FREE* ★ SOY-FREE OPTION**

My beloved local Indian restaurant has closed, so I'm turning to my slow cooker to get my curry fix. Indian food is easy to make at home once you have a few key spices in your arsenal. This way, you can have your favorite curries wherever you live! If you plan on cooking this recipe for longer than 8 hours, increase the amount of water to 1 cup (235 ml).

1½ cups (355 ml) crushed or puréed tomatoes

1½ cups (60 g) unsoaked soy curls (**use 1½ cups [246 g] cooked chickpeas for soy-free)

1 cup (110 g) potatoes, small dice

½ cup (120 ml) water

1 tablespoon (9 g) bell pepper, minced

2 teaspoons (5.4 g) fresh ginger, grated, divided

2 cloves garlic, minced, divided

½ teaspoon Garam Masala (page 21)

½ teaspoon whole mustard seeds

½ teaspoon whole cumin seeds

½ teaspoon crumbled fresh curry leaves, optional

¼ teaspoon ground turmeric

¼ teaspoon ground coriander

⅛ teaspoon ground cardamom

1 cup (56 g) minced greens (Kale, collards, mustard greens, and Swiss chard are my favorites, but feel free to use what you have on hand.)

1 to 2 tablespoons (15 to 30 g) vegan plain yogurt, vegan sour cream, **Cashew Cream (page 28), or *Extra-Thick Silken Tofu Sour Cream (page 28), optional

Salt, to taste (I used ¼ teaspoon gray sea salt.)

1½ to 3 cups (293 to 585 g) cooked basmati rice, for serving

Indian pickle on the side, optional

In the morning: Add the tomatoes, soy curls (or chickpeas), potatoes, water, bell pepper, 1 teaspoon ginger, 1 clove garlic, and the spices. You will use the rest of the garlic and ginger 30 minutes before serving to add a fresh burst of flavor that would otherwise fade away in long cooking times. Cook on low for 7 to 9 hours.

Thirty minutes before serving: Turn up to high. Add the rest of the garlic and ginger. Also stir in the greens, vegan yogurt (or substitute), and salt. Cook until the greens are tender, about 30 minutes. Serve with balsamic rice and Indian pickle.

YIELD: about 5 cups (965 g)

PER 1-CUP (193 G) SERVING (WITHOUT BROWN RICE): 108.9 calories; 3.1 g total fat; 0.4 g saturated fat; 6.6 g protein; 15.9 g carbohydrate; 4.3 g dietary fiber; 0 mg cholesterol

PREP TIME: 15 minutes

COOKING TIME: 7½ to 9½ hours

PEAR CHICKPEA FALL STEW

★ SOY-FREE   ★ OIL-FREE   ★ GLUTEN-FREE OPTION*

This stew is perfect for a romantic fall dinner. Try improvising with the ingredients you have on hand to keep this meal simple. This nutritious stew gets a slight sweetness from the pears and a brightness from the lemon that's grounded in the earthiness of the beets and greens.

1 pear, peeled and chopped

1 cup (164 g) cooked chickpeas

1 cup (235 ml) water

1 teaspoon vegan bouillon

1 carrot, diced

¼ cup (56 g) golden beet, diced

1 clove garlic, minced

1 bay leaf

½ teaspoon dried sage

1 sprig rosemary or ¼ teaspoon ground rosemary

1 teaspoon lemon juice or apple cider vinegar

½ to 1 cup (34 to 67 g) chopped fresh kale, (18 to 36 g) Swiss chard, or (15 to 30 g) spinach

Salt and pepper, to taste

Cooked whole-wheat couscous (*use brown rice couscous), for serving

In the morning: Add everything except the greens, salt, pepper, and couscous to the slow cooker. Cook on low for 7 to 9 hours.

Thirty minutes before serving: Turn up to high, add the amount of chopped greens that fit in your slow cooker, and cook until the greens are bright green and tender. Add salt and pepper to taste. Remove bay leaf. Serve over cooked couscous with a side salad.

YIELD: about 3 cups (580 g)
PER 1-CUP (193 G) SERVING (WITHOUT COUSCOUS): 148.9 calories; 1.2 g total fat; 0.1 g saturated fat; 5.4 g protein; 30.9 g carbohydrate; 6.7 g dietary fiber; 0 mg cholesterol
PREP TIME: 15 minutes
COOKING TIME: 7½ to 9½ hours

RECIPE VARIATION
You can use winter squash or sweet potato in place of the beet, apples instead of pears, and white beans instead of chickpeas.

NEW ORLEANS RED BEANS AND RICE

★ SOY-FREE OPTION** ★ GLUTEN-FREE OPTION* ★ OIL-FREE

This recipe for red beans calls for dried beans. The long cooking time allows the beans to get creamier, and using dried beans saves money, too! You can use canned kidney beans or precooked ones—just put the ingredients together in the morning instead of the night before and adjust the water down to 1 cup (235 ml).

1 cup (250 g) dry red beans (small red beans, not kidney beans)

3 cups (700 ml) water

2 cloves garlic, minced

2 bay leaves

1 teaspoon Cajun Spice Blend (page 23)

Few drops liquid smoke or smoked salt

Tabasco sauce, optional (to taste or serve on the side)

Salt, to taste

1½ to 3 cups (293 to 585 g) cooked brown rice for serving

1 or 2 vegan sausage links (*omit for gluten-free) or a slice of grilled tofu (**omit for soy-free)

The night before: Add the dried beans, water, garlic, and bay leaves to the slow cooker. Cook on low overnight.

In the morning: Add the Cajun seasoning, liquid smoke, Tabasco, if using, and ¼ to ½ cup (60 to 120 ml) of water depending on how long you will be gone for the day or if the beans look too dry to cook all day. You can cook these beans for a long time if you add extra water, so they are good for days when you know you will be coming home late.

Before serving, taste, and add salt and hot sauce, if desired. Remove bay leaves. Serve on a bed of cooked rice and place some of the optional grilled tofu or sausage links on top.

YIELD: about 3 cups (580 g)

PER 1-CUP (193 G) SERVING (WITHOUT BROWN RICE AND SAUSAGE OR TOFU): 222.1 calories; 0.9 g total fat; 0.1 g saturated fat; 13.6 g protein; 40.9 g carbohydrate; 16.4 g dietary fiber; 0 mg cholesterol

PREP TIME: 15 minutes

COOKING TIME: 7 to 9 hours

RECIPE VARIATIONS

- Serve with a side salad to add some fresh veggies and balance out the meal.
- If you only have kidney beans, you need to boil them on the stove for 10 minutes before adding them to the slow cooker. This is because kidney beans contain a toxic agent, phytohaemagglutinin, also known as kidney bean lectin.

THREE SISTERS STEW

★ SOY-FREE ★ GLUTEN-FREE ★ OIL-FREE

Many gardeners grow scarlet runner beans for their beautiful red flowers and green bean-like pods. But if you can keep yourself from eating the pods until the end of the season, you can harvest some beautiful beans to add to your pantry. Mine never make it that far, but ranchogordo.com has them dried, and also carries my favorite chili powder, to buy online.

FOR THE MORNING INGREDIENTS:

⅔ cup (122 g) dry scarlet runner beans, uncooked

2 cups (475 ml) water

1½ cups corn kernels, (231 g) fresh or (246 g) frozen

1 teaspoon cumin

½ teaspoon chili powder

FOR THE EVENING INGREDIENTS:

1 cup (120 g) summer squash, small dice

½ cup (90 g) diced tomatoes

Salt and pepper, to taste

More cumin and chili powder, as needed to taste

In the morning: Add all the morning ingredients to your small slow cooker and cook on low for 7 to 9 hours.

Thirty to 45 minutes before serving: Turn up to high. Add the veggies, salt, and pepper. Taste and add more cumin and chili powder if needed. (This will vary depending on cooking time and age of your spices.)

Cook until the summer squash is tender, about 30 minutes. Serve with a big piece of toasted crusty bread (*use gluten-free).

YIELD: about 4 cups (772 g)
PER 1-CUP (193 G) SERVING: 187.9 calories; 0.9 g total fat; 0.1 g saturated fat; 9.1 g protein; 37.9 g carbohydrate; 8.9 g dietary fiber; 0 mg cholesterol
PREP TIME: 15 minutes
COOKING TIME: 7½ to 9¾ hours

RECIPE VARIATIONS

- Try this recipe with other heirloom beans, such as tepary, which are actually native to North America, or even other beans that break down more, such as pintos and cranberry beans.
- You can also use canned kidney beans with ½ cup (120 ml) water and put everything (except for the salt and pepper) in the slow cooker on low all day. This will result in a thicker chili-like stew, but you can add more water if you would like a thinner consistency.

SPICY SOUTHERN CHICKPEAS AND GRITS

★ SOY-FREE   ★ GLUTEN-FREE   ★ OIL-FREE

This is my (vegan) version of shrimp and grits. Like many Southern dishes, there's bacon in the original, but my version contains liquid smoke. You get all of the flavor, plus it's cruelty-free!

1 can (16 ounces, or 455 g) or 1½ cups (246 g) cooked chickpeas

1 cup (150 g) bell pepper, chopped

1 can (14.5 ounces, or 410 g) or 1½ cups (270 g) diced tomatoes

½ cup (120 ml) water

2 teaspoons (4 g) Cajun Spice Blend (page 23)

¼ to ½ teaspoon chipotle powder

2 cloves garlic, minced

Few dashes liquid smoke or smoked salt

Tabasco or other hot sauce, optional

Salt and pepper, to taste

Add all ingredients, except for the salt and pepper, to the slow cooker and cook on low for 7 to 9 hours.

Before serving, taste, add salt and pepper, and then reseason to your liking. You may need to add more liquid smoke, Cajun seasoning, or chipotle. Serve over Slow Cooker Grits for Two (recipe follows).

YIELD: about 4½ cups (868 g)
PER 1-CUP (193 G) SERVING (WITHOUT GRITS): 126.8 calories; 0.9 g total fat; 0.1 g saturated fat; 5 g protein; 25.6 g carbohydrate; 6.5 g dietary fiber; 0 mg cholesterol
PREP TIME: 10 minutes
COOKING TIME: 7 to 9 hours

SLOW COOKER GRITS FOR TWO

★ SOY-FREE   ★ GLUTEN-FREE   ★ OIL-FREE

If you have two small slow cookers, you can cook these tasty grits while the chickpeas cook and come home to a complete meal!

½ cup (70 g) grits, yellow or white

1 cup (235 ml) unsweetened nondairy milk

1 cup (235 ml) water

1 veggie bouillon cube

Salt and pepper, to taste

Add all the ingredients to a slow cooker. Cook on low for 7 to 9 hours.

YIELD: about 2 cups (484 g)
PER 1-CUP (242 G) SERVING: 104 calories; 1.8 g total fat; 0 g saturated fat; 2.0 g protein; 14.5 g carbohydrate; 1.5 g dietary fiber; 0 mg cholesterol
PREP TIME: 5 minutes
COOKING TIME: 7 to 9 hours

CLEAN-OUT-THE-FRIDGE VEGGIE CURRY

★SOY-FREE   ★GLUTEN-FREE   ★OIL-FREE

You can incorporate any veggies you need to use up in this dish, so it's a perfect dinner the night before you go to the grocery store or farmers' market. Plus, it's always a treat to eat Indian food in your own home!

1 cup (100 g) green beans

1 cup (110 g) chopped potatoes

½ cup (50 g) cauliflower in small florets

½ cup (120 ml) water

¼ cup (33 g) diced carrots

¼ cup (25 g) sliced okra

1 clove garlic, minced

1 tablespoon (8 g) grated ginger

½ teaspoon Garam Masala (page 21)

½ teaspoon whole mustard seeds

¼ teaspoon turmeric

¼ teaspoon cumin

¼ teaspoon coriander

¼ teaspoon cardamom

Salt, to taste

Add everything except for the salt to your slow cooker and cook on low for 7 to 9 hours.

Mix in the salt, taste, and adjust spices. Serve with vegan naan, roti, or basmati rice.

YIELD: about 3½ cups (675 g)

PER 1-CUP (193 G) SERVING: 77.4 calories; 0.1 g total fat; 0 g saturated fat; 2.2 g protein; 17.9 g carbohydrate; 4.0 g dietary fiber; 0 mg cholesterol

PREP TIME: 15 minutes

COOKING TIME: 7 to 9 hours

RECIPE VARIATION
Make a quick raita by combining 8 ounces (225 g) unsweetened nondairy yogurt, ½ a minced cucumber, and ½ a shredded carrot to serve alongside.

MOTHER STALLARD BEAN AND BARLEY STEW

★ SOY-FREE   ★ OIL-FREE

This stew, filled with firm, football-shaped Mother Stallard beans, is made even more wholesome with the addition of barley, sweet potato, and your choice of root veggie. The flavors meld into a great broth that's brightened with tomatoes and a hint of sweet balsamic vinegar. Believe it or not, kids love it!

FOR THE MORNING INGREDIENTS:

3 cups (700 ml) water

½ cup (97 g) Mother Stallard beans or pinto beans

½ cup (92 g) barley

½ cup (78 g) celery root, (75 g) turnip, or (55 g) potato

½ cup (67 g) sweet potato

2 cloves garlic, minced

2 vegan bouillon cubes

FOR THE EVENING INGREDIENTS:

1 cup (180 g) diced tomatoes

1 teaspoon balsamic vinegar (Juniper berry balsamic is amazing, but plain works great, too.)

Salt, to taste

In the morning: Add all the morning ingredients to your slow cooker and cook on low for 7 to 9 hours.

Thirty minutes before serving: Add the tomatoes, balsamic vinegar, and salt, to taste.

YIELD: about 5 cups (965 g)

PER 1-CUP (193 G) SERVING: 125.6 calories; 0.4 g total fat; 0.1 g saturated fat; 4.3 g protein; 26.5 g carbohydrate; 5.6 g dietary fiber; 0 mg cholesterol

PREP TIME: 15 minutes

COOKING TIME: 7½ to 9½ hours

RECIPE VARIATION

Feel free to substitute a gluten-free grain like brown rice or oat groats to make this gluten-free.

TOMATILLO AND WHITE BEAN CHILI

★ SOY-FREE   ★ GLUTEN-FREE   ★ OIL-FREE

This chili comes together in a flash and is perfect to throw in the slow cooker before you leave for work. It's great served as is in a bowl, but it's also nice in burritos or tacos. I love the tanginess of the tomatillos in this mild stew. You can always spice it up with a few minced jalapeños if you prefer your chili fiery.

1½ cups (269 g) cooked or 1 can (15 ounces, or 420 g) white beans, rinsed and drained

1 cup (132 g) diced tomatillo (about 8 medium)

3 cloves garlic, minced

1 heaping tablespoon (10 g) green chiles

½ teaspoon dried marjoram

½ teaspoon dried oregano

⅛ teaspoon cumin powder

Salt and pepper, to taste

1 tablespoon (1 g) minced fresh cilantro, for garnish

Add all the ingredients except the salt and pepper to the slow cooker and cook on low for 7 to 9 hours. Before serving, add salt and pepper. Taste and adjust any of the seasonings as needed.

YIELD: about 3 cups (580 g)
PER 1-CUP (193 G) SERVING: 63.5 calories; 0.9 g total fat; 0.1 g saturated fat; 3.1 g protein; 8.3 g carbohydrate; 3.8 g dietary fiber; 0 mg cholesterol
PREP TIME: 15 minutes
COOKING TIME: 7 to 9 hours

RECIPE VARIATION
Can't find tomatillos where you are? Go ahead and substitute regular tomatoes.

DID YOU KNOW?
If you are avoiding gluten because of allergies, be sure to look on the packages of all grains for the gluten-free labels. Even grits and oats can be cross-contaminated with gluten-containing products in a manufacturing plant.

WACKY CINCINNATI CHILI

★ OIL-FREE OPTION* ★ SOY-FREE OPTION** ★ GLUTEN-FREE OPTION***

Cincinnati chili is similar to a regular meaty chili except it has spices that you see more in pumpkin pie than in an all-American stew. Traditionally, it's a meat chili that has kidney beans as an optional topping, as well as shredded cheese and onions.
Then, oddly enough, it's served over pasta.

FOR THE MORNING INGREDIENTS:

¾ cup (144 g) dry black beluga lentils (You can sub in other lentils; the chili just won't be as dark.)

1½ cups (355 ml) water

2 cloves garlic, minced

½ cup (55 g) ground vegan crumbles, either store-bought or Make-Your-Own Gluten Crumbles (page 18) or use ½ cup (87 g) cooked quinoa for soy-free** and gluten-free***

1 bay leaf

½ teaspoon ground cumin

¼ teaspoon ground hot pepper, such as chipotle

⅛ teaspoon ground cinnamon

1 teaspoon chili powder

1 teaspoon cocoa powder

Pinch ground allspice

Ground hot pepper of choice, to taste, optional

FOR THE EVENING INGREDIENTS:

1½ cups (270 g) diced tomatoes

Dash freshly ground nutmeg

Salt, to taste

2 to 3 cups (270 to 405 g) cooked pasta, for serving (***use gluten-free)

Traditional toppings, all optional: shredded vegan cheese (*omit for oil free), chopped onions, and cooked kidney beans

In the morning: Add all the morning ingredients to the slow cooker. Cook for 7 to 9 hours on low.

Thirty minutes before serving: Add tomatoes and nutmeg, taste, add salt, and adjust other seasonings as needed. Turn to high and cook 30 minutes more to incorporate the tomatoes into the chili.

Remove bay leaf before serving. Serve over cooked pasta and top with your choice of toppings.

YIELD: about 3 cups (580 g)
PER 1-CUP (193 G) SERVING (WITHOUT PASTA OR EXTRAS): 181 calories; 1.9 g total fat; 0 g saturated fat; 7.4 g protein; 31.5 g carbohydrate; 4.6 g dietary fiber; 0 mg cholesterol
PREP TIME: 10 minutes
COOKING TIME: 7½ to 9½ hours

RECIPE VARIATION

For Halloween, I serve this dish over spinach pasta with a vegan cheez ghost cut out with a cookie cutter. I use black sesame seeds for the eyes. Spooky!

HEIRLOOM BEAN CHILI POWERED UP WITH ANCIENT GRAINS

★ SOY-FREE   ★ GLUTEN-FREE   ★ OIL-FREE

If you don't eat soy or seitan but are looking for a hearty chili, give this one a go. The millet and amaranth thicken up the chili and give it a great texture. You can use regular beans, but I've listed some heirlooms for you to try if you feel like you're in a bean rut. But don't let the unusual names scare you—they are delicious.

FOR THE MORNING INGREDIENTS:

3 cups (700 ml) water

¼ cup (33 g) sweet potato, chopped small

¼ cup (50 g) dry moro or black beans

¼ cup (50 g) dry sange de toro or pinto beans

¼ cup (50 g) dry alubia blanca or white beans

¼ cup (50 g) millet

⅛ cup (26 g) amaranth

2 cloves garlic, minced

½ teaspoon chili powder

½ teaspoon cumin powder

FOR THE EVENING INGREDIENTS:

2 tablespoons (32 g) tomato paste

1 teaspoon dried oregano

¼ teaspoon chili powder

¼ teaspoon cumin powder

Salt and pepper

In the morning: Add all the morning ingredients and cook on low for 7 to 9 hours.

Thirty minutes before serving: Add the tomato paste, oregano, chili powder, and cumin to the slow cooker and mix well. Cook on low for 30 minutes. (If the tomato paste was frozen, turn the slow cooker to high.)

Before serving, add salt and pepper. Taste and adjust any of the seasonings as needed.

YIELD: about 5 cups (965 g)
PER 1-CUP (193 G) SERVING: 81.9 calories; 0.6 g total fat; 0.1 g saturated fat; 4.0 g protein; 15.5 g carbohydrate; 2.7 g dietary fiber; 0 mg cholesterol
PREP TIME: 15 minutes
COOKING TIME: 7½ to 9½ hours

DID YOU KNOW?

What the heck are moro beans, sange de toro beans, and alubia blanca beans? They are fancy schmancy heirloom beans. You will not find them in your local grocery store and maybe not even at your health food store. Try ranchogordo.com—it can fulfill all your heirloom bean needs.

TAMARIND TEMPEH

★ GLUTEN-FREE   ★ OIL-FREE

This is an Indian dish that leans toward the sour side of the taste spectrum.
It's a perfect change of pace from the usual curries. If you are avoiding soy,
try making it with seitan instead of tempeh or even use precooked chickpeas.

8 ounces (225 g) tempeh, cubed

1 cup (140 g) cubed winter squash

1 cup (180 g) diced tomatoes

½ cup (120 ml) water

¼ cup (22 g) cooked onion
(page 19)

2 cloves garlic, minced

1 tablespoon (16 g) tamarind paste

1 teaspoon grated fresh ginger

1 teaspoon ground turmeric

1 teaspoon ground coriander

½ to 1 teaspoon chili powder

¼ teaspoon ground cumin

Salt, to taste

Add everything except for the salt to your slow cooker and cook on low for 7 to 9 hours.

Add salt before serving, taste, and adjust spices as needed. Serve over steamed rice.

YIELD: about 4 cups (772 g)
PER 1-CUP (193 G) SERVING: 153.7 calories; 6.4 g total fat; 2.3 g saturated fat; 11.7 g protein; 16.2 g carbohydrate; 3.0 g dietary fiber; 0 mg cholesterol
PREP TIME: 10 minutes
COOKING TIME: 7 to 9 hours

RECIPE VARIATION
If you aren't so sure you'll like the sour taste of tamarind paste, start with half the amount. You can taste it before serving and add more if you're comfortable with it.

POTATO CAULIFLOWER CURRY (ALOO GOBI)

★ SOY-FREE   ★ GLUTEN-FREE OPTION*   ★ OIL-FREE

Nothing is more comforting than a main dish with potatoes and cauliflower. It's such a simple dish, but the blend of spices makes it taste really exotic. I love the way the black cardamom pods make it a little bit smoky and the ginger mellows out with the coriander. Serve with Indian bread (*use gluten-free) over balsamic rice.

1½ cups (165 g) potatoes, cut in chunks

1½ cups (150 g) cauliflower, broken into florets

1 cup (180 g) tomatoes

¼ cup (60 ml) water

¼ cup (22 g) cooked onion (page 19)

2 cloves garlic, minced

1½ teaspoons (4 g) grated ginger

2 whole black cardamom pods

½ teaspoon whole cumin seeds

½ teaspoon ground turmeric

¼ teaspoon ground coriander

¼ teaspoon chili powder

Pinch ground cloves

Salt, to taste

¼ cup (4 g) fresh chopped cilantro

Add everything except the salt and cilantro to the slow cooker and cook on low for 7 to 9 hours. Remove cardamom pods. Before serving, add the salt to taste and mix in the fresh cilantro.

YIELD: about 4 cups (772 g)
PER 1-CUP (193 G) SERVING: 68.8 calories; 0.3 g total fat; 0.1 g saturated fat; 2.5 g protein; 15.4 g carbohydrate; 2.9 g dietary fiber; 0 mg cholesterol
PREP TIME: 15 minutes
COOKING TIME: 7 to 9 hours

RECIPE VARIATION
Switch out the potato for turnips or the cauliflower for cabbage or any other in-season vegetable. This dish is good year-round using whatever you have in the fridge.

CREAMY VEGGIE CURRY (NAVRATAN KORMA)

★ SOY-FREE OPTION*   ★ GLUTEN-FREE   ★ OIL-FREE OPTION**

Navratan Korma is a creamy curry full of veggies, dried fruit, and usually cashews. I'm putting the cashews in via Cashew Cream, which thickens it up just right. It's a decadent dish that even curry haters will love.

1 cup (100 g) cauliflower florets or (110 g) diced potato

1 cup (130 g) chopped carrots or (140 g) winter squash

½ cup (75 g) peas or (50 g) green beans

½ cup (90 g) diced tomatoes

½ cup (120 ml) water

¼ cup (22 g) cooked onion (page 19)

2 tablespoons (19 g) minced bell pepper

1 tablespoon (8 g) grated ginger

½ teaspoon ground turmeric

½ teaspoon ground coriander

¼ teaspoon chili powder

1 tablespoon (9 g) raisins

¼ cup (60 ml) nondairy milk

2 tablespoons (30 g) *Cashew Cream (page 28), vegan sour cream, or **Extra-Thick Silken Tofu Sour Cream (page 28)

Salt, to taste

1½ to 3 cups (293 to 585 g) basmati rice, for serving

Add everything except the milk, cashew cream, and salt to the slow cooker. Cook on low for 7 to 9 hours.

Before serving, add milk and Cashew Cream (or substitute) and mix well. Add salt to taste. Serve over steamed basmati rice.

YIELD: about 3 cups (580 g)

PER 1-CUP (193 G) SERVING (WITHOUT RICE): 96 calories; 2.5 g total fat; 0.8 g saturated fat; 3 g protein; 17.6 g carbohydrate; 4.5 g dietary fiber; 0 mg cholesterol

PREP TIME: 15 minutes

COOKING TIME: 7 to 9 hours

DID YOU KNOW?

Many Indian recipes use yogurt, cream, and ghee, which is clarified butter. When you're eating at a new-to-you Indian restaurant, be sure to ask questions to ensure you're ordering vegan. Navratan Korma is usually not vegan if you don't make it at home.

YELLOW LENTIL STEW (DAL)

★ SOY-FREE ★ GLUTEN-FREE OPTION* ★ OIL-FREE

Dal is an Indian lentil dish that is so varied in types of lentils and flavors that you may not have eaten the same one twice. If you have an Indian store nearby, go there for beans and spices. If not, you can find most beans online and have them shipped right to your door!

3½ cups (820 ml) cups water

½ cup (96 g) masoor dal or red lentils

½ cup (96 g) channa dal or split baby chickpeas

¼ cup (48 g) moong dal or golden lentils

2 black cardamom pods

2 whole dried red chiles

2 cloves garlic, minced

½ teaspoon cumin seeds

½ teaspoon mustard seeds

½ teaspoon ground turmeric

¼ teaspoon ground cinnamon

1 tablespoon (2.5 g) fresh curry leaves or 1 teaspoon dried, optional

Salt, to taste

Add everything except for the curry leaves and salt to your slow cooker. Cook on low for 7 to 9 hours.

Mix in the curry leaves and salt. Remove cardamom pods and whole chiles. Serve with Indian bread (*use gluten-free) or basmati rice.

YIELD: about 4 cups (772 g)
PER 1-CUP (193 G) SERVING: 201.6 calories; 2.0 g total fat; 0 g saturated fat; 11.7 g protein; 31.5 g carbohydrate; 7.8 g dietary fiber; 0 mg cholesterol
PREP TIME: 15 minutes
COOKING TIME: 7 to 9 hours

RECIPE VARIATION
Dress up this dal with minced greens, green beans, or summer squash by adding these quick-cooking vegetables in the last 30 minutes of cooking. My friend Kalpana always has a new dal variation up her sleeve!

THAI MASSAMAN CURRY

★ SOY-FREE   ★ GLUTEN-FREE   ★ OIL-FREE

You may be familiar with Thai green and red curries. Massaman curry uses many of the same ingredients but adds cinnamon, cloves, nutmeg, and cumin to give it a totally different feel. Don't worry—there's still rich creamy coconut milk in it, too. These other spices just add a little bit of traditional Indian flavors to it.

FOR THE MORNING INGREDIENTS:

½ cup (120 ml) water

1 cup (110 g) diced potato

1 small carrot, diced

1 cup (120 g) summer squash (green, yellow, or a mix), cut into medium chunks

¼ cup (38 g) chopped bell pepper

1 teaspoon kaffir lime leaves or lime zest

1 teaspoon minced fresh gangala or fresh ginger

1 teaspoon tamarind paste

1 teaspoon coriander seeds

½ teaspoon lemongrass or other lemon herb such as verbena or balm

½ teaspoon chili powder or fresh minced chile

¼ teaspoon each cumin, nutmeg, cinnamon, and cardamom

⅛ teaspoon ground cloves

FOR THE EVENING INGREDIENTS:

Juice of ½ lime

1 can (14 ounces, or 410 ml) light coconut milk

1½ to 3 cups (293 to 585 g) steamed rice, for serving

In the morning: Add everything except the lime and coconut milk to your slow cooker. Cook on low for 7 to 9 hours.

Thirty minutes before serving: Add the lime juice and coconut milk. Turn up to high and cook until heated thoroughly. Serve over steamed rice—jasmine rice is my favorite with this dish.

YIELD: about 3 cups (772 g)
PER 1-CUP (257 G) SERVING (WITHOUT RICE): 177.2 calories; 9.5 g total fat; "7.0 g saturated fat; 4.2 g protein; 18.7 g carbohydrate; 2.2 g dietary fiber; 0 mg cholesterol
PREP TIME: 15 minutes
COOKING TIME: 7½ to 9½ hours

DID YOU KNOW?
Don't panic when this looks a little browner than other Thai curries—the color is from the spices. It will still have a coconutty taste.

—CHAPTER SEVEN—

TASTY FILLINGS:
SANDWICHES, TACOS, AND MORE

EVERY ONCE IN A WHILE YOU NEED A BREAK FROM SOUPS AND STEWS, or you need a meal that's a little more casual for the perfect summer dinner outside. These warm sandwich (and taco) fillings are easy to make in your little slow cooker, and they can cook while you're at work or out having fun. Soy curl barbeque, a few lentil tacos, mushroom sliders, or a Cajun-inspired black-eyed pea sloppy joe can add some spice back into your dinners. It certainly doesn't hurt that they are ready when you walk in the door hungry!

CAROLINA BARBECUE SOY CURLS

★ OIL-FREE   ★ SOY-FREE OPTION*   ★ GLUTEN-FREE OPTION**

Every region has a barbecue that's associated with it. Where I live in North Carolina, vinegar plays a big part. I like my barbecue tempered with a little brown sugar and tomato paste, as in this recipe. Plus, I threw in a little hard cider for good measure. Of course, you can use plain apple cider to keep this dish alcohol-free.

FOR THE SAUCE:

¾ cup (175 ml) water

½ cup (120 ml) hard cider

¼ cup (60 ml) apple cider vinegar

2 cloves garlic, minced

2 tablespoons (30 g) brown sugar

1 tablespoon (16 g) tomato paste

¼ teaspoon liquid smoke

¼ teaspoon salt

¼ teaspoon black pepper

⅛ teaspoon dry mustard

Pinch to ¼ teaspoon red pepper, to suit your hotness level

FOR THE BARBECUE:

1 cup (40 g) soy curls (*use Make-Your-Own Gluten Crumbles on page 18 for soy-free)

2 or 3 buns, for serving (**use gluten-free)

Mix all the sauce ingredients together in the slow cooker. The sauce will be watery at this point but will thicken while it cooks all day. Stir in the soy curls (or Make-Your-Own Gluten Crumbles, page 18) and cook on low for 7 to 9 hours.

Serve on a toasted bun. If you want the whole North Carolina experience, add some vegan coleslaw on top of the barbecue in your sandwich.

YIELD: about 2 cups (386 g)
PER 1-CUP (193 G) SERVING (WITHOUT BUN): 156.5 calories; 3.0 g total fat; 0 g saturated fat; 7.4 g protein; 25.9 g carbohydrate; 2.3 g dietary fiber; 0 mg cholesterol
PREP TIME: 15 minutes
COOKING TIME: 7 to 9 hours

RECIPE VARIATION

If you don't have any hard cider on hand, use apple cider or even apple juice in its place. The sauce may be just a touch sweeter, but it will still go great in this vinegar-based barbecue.

LENTIL QUINOA TACO FILLING

★ SOY-FREE   ★ GLUTEN-FREE OPTION*   ★ OIL-FREE

This recipe contains no soy or gluten yet has an almost meaty texture that taco lovers love. This filling is also a great place to stash some shredded greens, fresh chopped summer squash, and more seasonal goodies from your market. You can cook them with the filling below or add them raw to freshen it up a bit. Let your imagination guide you.

¼ cup (48 g) brown lentils

¼ cup (48 g) beluga lentils or brown lentils

¼ cup (43 g) quinoa, rinsed

2 cups (475 ml) water

2 cloves garlic, minced

½ teaspoon chili powder

½ teaspoon smoked paprika

Salt and pepper, to taste

6 soft or hard corn taco shells (*use gluten-free)

EXTRAS:

Shredded lettuce

Diced tomatoes

Vegan sour cream substitute

Salsa

Or any other of your favorite taco toppings

Add all the ingredients except the salt, pepper, and taco shells to the slow cooker and cook on low for 7 to 9 hours. Before serving, add salt and pepper. Taste and adjust any of the seasonings as needed.

Serve in taco shells with lettuce, tomatoes, vegan sour cream substitute, salsa, or any of your other favorite taco toppings.

YIELD: about 6 tacos

PER ½-CUP (100 G) SERVING (WITHOUT TACO SHELL): 49.3 calories; 0.5 g total fat; 0 g saturated fat; 2.6 g protein; 8.8 g carbohydrate; 1.8 g dietary fiber; 0 mg cholesterol

PREP TIME: 15 minutes

COOKING TIME: 7 to 9 hours

DID YOU KNOW?

You can add texture to a dish even if you are cooking for people who do not eat soy or gluten. Just add quinoa, millet, or amaranth to your recipe with enough extra liquid to cook them in. Add the grains individually or in a combination to make your plant-based meal extra-hearty.

SLOPPY BLACK-EYED PEAS

★ SOY-FREE ★ OIL-FREE ★ GLUTEN-FREE OPTION*

The black-eyed peas cook down into a thick stew as they meld with the Cajun seasoning and veggies to create a New Orleans–inspired sloppy joe. It's great inside a bun or ladled over an open-faced bun (*use gluten-free). It's one of my favorite recipes!

FOR THE MORNING INGREDIENTS:

2 cups (475 ml) water

⅓ cup (48 g) dry black-eyed peas

⅓ cup (43 g) carrots, chopped

⅙ cup (33 g) millet

2 tablespoons (19 g) minced bell pepper

1 clove garlic, minced

1 teaspoon Cajun seasoning

⅛ to ¼ teaspoon liquid smoke, to taste

FOR THE EVENING INGREDIENTS:

1 cup (56 g) minced greens (collards, kale, etc.)

2 tablespoons (32 g) tomato paste

Salt and pepper, to taste

2 or 3 buns, for serving (*use gluten-free)

In the morning: Add all the morning ingredients to the slow cooker and cook on low for 7 to 9 hours.

Thirty minutes before serving: Add the greens and tomato paste. Add the salt and pepper right before serving and more Cajun seasoning if needed. Serve open-faced style with the black-eyed pea mixture ladled over a lightly toasted bun.

YIELD: about 2½ cups (483 g)
PER 1-CUP (193 G) SERVING (WITHOUT BUN): 195.6 calories; 2.0 g total fat; 0 g saturated fat; 7.4 g protein; 38.5 g carbohydrate; 6.2 g dietary fiber; 0 mg cholesterol
PREP TIME: 15 minutes
COOKING TIME: 7½ to 9½ hours

RECIPE VARIATION
Use yellow-eyed peas, field peas, or other fresh shelled beans you find at the farmers' market to change these up from time to time.

DID YOU KNOW?
Millet has a slightly sweet taste and adds some extra iron and protein to your sloppy joe.

INDIAN MASHED VEGGIE SANDWICH (PAV BHAJI)

★ SOY-FREE   ★ OIL-FREE   ★ GLUTEN-FREE OPTION*

Pav is an Indian yeast roll that looks a lot like a slider bun. Bhaji is the spiced mashed vegetable mixture you put in it. If it's new to you, you're in for a delicious and filling treat!

2 cups (220 g) peeled and diced potatoes

1 cup (100 g) diced cauliflower

½ cup (120 ml) water

¼ cup (38 g) diced bell pepper

¼ cup green peas, (38 g) fresh or (33 g) frozen

1 cup (180 g) diced tomatoes

2 cloves garlic, minced

2 teaspoons (5.4 g) grated ginger

½ teaspoon ground coriander

½ teaspoon ground turmeric

½ teaspoon chili powder

⅛ teaspoon fennel seeds

¼ teaspoon ground cinnamon

Salt, to taste

Chopped cilantro, for garnish

4 toasted buns, for serving (*use gluten-free)

Add the diced potatoes through cinnamon to your slow cooker and cook on low for 7 to 9 hours.

Before serving, mash the cooked mixture with a potato masher or the back of a large wooden spoon. Add salt to taste. Spoon into a toasted bun and top with cilantro.

YIELD: about 4 cups (900 g)
PER 1-CUP (225 G) SERVING (WITHOUT BUN): 85.8 calories; 0.3 g total fat; 0.1 g saturated fat; 3.1 g protein; 19.0 g carbohydrate; 3.3 g dietary fiber; 0 mg cholesterol
PREP TIME: 15 minutes
COOKING TIME: 7 to 9 hours

RECIPE VARIATION
Use leftovers as a cracker or pappadam spread for an exotic twist at your next party.

NEW ENGLAND TOFU ROLLS

★ OIL-FREE   ★ GLUTEN-FREE OPTION*

In this recipe, the tofu cooks all day, absorbing all the flavors from the seasoning.
Then you mix it with a little vegan mayo and lemon juice and serve it hot or cold on a roll.
Old Bay and similar seasoning blends are a mixture of ground bay leaves, celery salt, and black
and red pepper mixed with a few unexpected spices including ginger, cloves, and allspice.
That makes the flavor a little sweet and a little savory with a spicy bite at the end.

1 block (16 ounces, or 454 g) firm tofu, pressed and cubed

2 tablespoons (14 g) Old Bay or crab boil seasoning

½ cup (120 ml) water

¼ cup (60 g) vegan mayo or unsweetened vegan yogurt

¼ cup (25 g) minced celery

1 teaspoon minced chives

2 teaspoons (10 ml) lemon juice

Salt and pepper, to taste

6 toasted hot dog buns, for serving (*use gluten-free)

Add the cubed tofu, Old Bay seasoning, and water to the slow cooker and cook on low for 7 to 9 hours.

Remove the tofu from the slow cooker with a slotted spoon and put it in a medium mixing bowl. Add the mayo, celery, chives, and lemon juice and combine. Add a few tablespoons (45 to 60 ml) of the cooking broth to thin the mixture, if needed. Taste, add salt and pepper, and then adjust seasonings. (Old Bay and most crab boil mixes have salt, so keep that in mind when adjusting seasonings.)

Serve in toasted hot dog buns.

YIELD: 3 servings that fill 2 buns per serving

PER 1-CUP (193 G) SERVING (WITHOUT BUNS): 134.0 calories; 14.1 g total fat; 1.5 g saturated fat; 17.1 g protein; 5.0 g carbohydrate; 2.7 g dietary fiber; 0 mg cholesterol

PREP TIME: 15 minutes

COOKING TIME: 7 to 9 hours

DID YOU KNOW?
I love the smell of Old Bay seasoning. It's vegan and lends a nice spicy flavor to the tofu sandwich. It is quite salty, however, so look for the salt-free version if you are on a low-sodium diet.

ASIAN SHIITAKE SLIDERS

★ SOY-FREE OPTION*   ★ GLUTEN-FREE OPTION**

These sliders are a little sweet, a little spicy, and the perfect fuss-free meal.
Just make sure you have some mini-buns or dinner rolls (**use gluten-free) on hand. The
mushroom caps are like little burgers bathed in a delicious, Asian-inspired sauce.

FOR THE SAUCE:

⅔ cup (160 ml) water

3 teaspoons (20 g) orange
marmalade or apricot preserves

1 teaspoon cooked onion (page 19),
minced

1 teaspoon sesame oil

1 teaspoon hoisin sauce

1 teaspoon vegan Worcestershire
sauce

1 teaspoon rice wine vinegar

1 teaspoon low-sodium soy sauce
(*use coconut aminos for soy-free
or **gluten-free)

½ teaspoon Sriracha

8 ounces (225 g) shiitake
mushrooms, stems removed

6 to 8 slider rolls or dinner rolls,
for serving (**use gluten-free)

Mix all the sauce ingredients together in a bowl. Layer the mushroom caps in the crock and then pour the marinade over them. Cook on low for 7 to 9 hours.

Use tongs to fish out a mushroom cap per slider. If they are small, you may need up to three per slider. Then drizzle some of the tasty sauce on the bun or directly on the mushrooms. I like my sliders just like that, but you could top with a mixture of shredded cabbage and carrots to dress it up.

YIELD: about 6 sliders
PER SLIDER (WITHOUT BUN): 25.6 calories; 0 g total fat; 0 g saturated fat; 0.8 g protein; 5.6 g carbohydrate; 0.4 g dietary fiber; 0 mg cholesterol
PREP TIME: 15 minutes
COOKING TIME: 7 to 9 hours

RECIPE VARIATION

Make this recipe soy-free by using coconut aminos instead of soy sauce or gluten-free by using gluten-free soy sauce and gluten-free bread. If you'd like a thick sauce, take out the cooked mushrooms and set aside. Then go ahead and turn the slow cooker to high and mix in cornstarch or flour about ½ teaspoon at a time until the mixture thickens, mixing well after each addition.

CHAPTER EIGHT

FAMILY FAVORITES:
ONE-POT PASTAS, RISOTTOS, AND PASTA SAUCES

THIS CHAPTER INCLUDES long-cooking barley risottos, quick-cooking pastas, and even a pasta sauce you can make ahead and freeze for nights you aren't able to plan ahead for.

Rice risottos are easy to make in the slow cooker and have a quick cooking time. I also included two barley risottos because they can handle cooking all day without breaking down—something that's not possible in a traditional rice risotto.

It's a great feeling when you know every ingredient that goes into your meal. It's even better when that meal has all your favorite flavors, too!

CHEEZY BUTTERNUT SQUASH MACARONI

★ OIL FREE   ★ SOY-FREE   ★ GLUTEN-FREE OPTION*

This is mac 'n' cheez that's all grown up. It's covered with a rich butternut squash and nutritional yeast sauce that's as nutritious as it is delicious.

FOR THE MORNING INGREDIENTS:

1½ cups (210 g) cubed butternut squash or other winter squash

½ cup (90 g) chopped tomatoes

1½ cups (355 ml) water

2 cloves garlic, minced

Three 3-inch (7.5 cm) sprigs fresh thyme or 1½ teaspoons (1.5 g) dried thyme

One 2-inch (5 cm) sprig fresh rosemary or ½ teaspoon dried rosemary

FOR THE EVENING INGREDIENTS:

¼ cup (24 g) nutritional yeast flakes

½ to 1 cup (120 to 235 ml) unsweetened nondairy milk

1½ cups (158 g) uncooked whole-wheat macaroni (*use gluten-free)

Salt and pepper, to taste

In the morning: Add the morning ingredients to the slow cooker. Cook on low for 7 to 9 hours.

Thirty to 45 minutes before serving: Purée the contents of the slow cooker in a blender with the nutritional yeast and ½ cup (120 ml) of the nondairy milk. Add the mixture back into the slow cooker and turn it up to high. Stir in the macaroni, cover, and cook for 20 minutes.

Stir well and add more milk if the sauce is getting too thick. Cook for 15 to 25 minutes more or until the pasta is al dente. Add salt and pepper to taste.

Make sure to check on the pasta every 10 minutes or so until you get good at gauging how fast it will cook in your slow cooker. It cooks faster in the smaller slow cooker.

YIELD: about 5 cups (700 g)
PER 1-CUP (140 G) SERVING: 168.2 calories; 1.1 g total fat; 0.1 g saturated fat; 6.9 g protein; 33.7 g carbohydrate; 5.9 g dietary fiber; 0 mg cholesterol
PREP TIME: 15 minutes
COOKING TIME: 7½ to 9¾ hours

RECIPE VARIATION
Make this dish even healthier by adding in some chopped greens or fresh broccoli. You can't have too much of this good thing.

HEARTY LASAGNA LAYERED WITH NUT RICOTTA

★ SOY-FREE   ★ GLUTEN-FREE OPTION*   ★ OIL-FREE OPTION**

This quick-to-make fast-cooking lasagna is filled with a rich nut ricotta and hearty seitan (or tempeh) crumbles. This will not serve up as pretty as a baked lasagna, but it will still make your family's faces light up!

FOR THE SAUCE:

2 cups (360 g) crushed tomatoes

1 teaspoon dried oregano

1 teaspoon dried basil

1 teaspoon agave nectar or ¼ teaspoon stevia

¼ teaspoon crushed red pepper

Salt and pepper, to taste

⅓ of a box (9 ounces, or 255 g) of whole-wheat lasagna noodles (*use gluten-free noodles)

1½ cups (390 g) Nut Ricotta (with fresh basil, if possible) (page 25)

1 cup (110 g) ground seitan crumbles, store-bought vegan Italian sausage, or Make-Your-Own Gluten Crumbles (page 18) (*use crumbled steamed tempeh)

¼ cup (28 g) shredded vegan mozzarella, optional**

Mix the all the sauce ingredients together except for the salt and pepper. Then add salt and pepper to suit your taste. Keep in mind if you are using commercial crumbles they will already be salted.

Spray the crock to make cleanup easier (**or line with parchment paper). Layer the lasagna as follows:

Spread a few tablespoons (33 to 44 g) of the sauce on the bottom of the crock.

Sprinkle a few tablespoons (21 to 28 g) of the crumbles on top of the sauce.

Break lasagna noodles to fit into the slow cooker and add a layer.

Spread a few tablespoons (48 to 64 g) of the nut ricotta on the noodles.

Repeat until all the ingredients are used, making sure to end with a layer of noodles covered with sauce.

If you have any leftover sauce, go ahead and pour it on the top. Cook on high for 1 to 2 hours or until the noodles are al dente. If desired, sprinkle the top with shredded vegan mozzarella and cook 10 minutes more.

YIELD: 4 small servings

PER SERVING: 476.7 calories; 22.6 g total fat; 0 g saturated fat; 29.4 g protein; 43.7 g carbohydrate; 7.3 g dietary fiber; 0 mg cholesterol

PREP TIME: 15 minutes

COOKING TIME: 1 to 2 hours

RECIPE VARIATION

Leave out the crumbles and add a mix of chopped eggplant, summer squash, bell peppers, and carrots for a veggie-rific pasta dish.

MUSHROOM BOURGUIGNON WITH PASTA

★ SOY-FREE ★ OIL-FREE ★ GLUTEN-FREE OPTION*

This dish is rich with mushrooms, and they cook down with the red wine and tomato paste to make a luxurious sauce. It's an easy grown-up dinner that's a treat to come home to.

2 tablespoons (11 g) cooked onion (page 19)

2 small carrots, cut into thick coins (about ¾ cup [98 g])

1 cup (70 g) mushrooms, cubed

½ cup (120 ml) red wine

1 tablespoon (16 g) tomato paste

2 cups (475 ml) water

Four 3-inch (7.5 cm) sprigs thyme

1 tablespoon (6 g) fresh marjoram or 1 teaspoon dried marjoram

1½ cups (158 g) small pasta shapes (*use gluten-free)

Salt and pepper, to taste

Add the onions, carrots, mushrooms, wine, tomato paste, water, and herbs to the slow cooker. Cook on low for 7 to 9 hours.

Twenty to 40 minutes before serving: Turn the slow cooker to high and stir in the dry pasta. It will take twice as long to cook whole-wheat pasta, so factor that in. Check it after about 15 minutes and stir. Serve just as the pasta becomes al dente.

YIELD: about 4½ cups (608 g)
PER 1-CUP (135 G) SERVING: 357.2 calories; 1.9 g total fat; 0 g saturated fat; 10.1 g protein; 68.8 g carbohydrate; 4.0 g dietary fiber; 0 mg cholesterol
PREP TIME: 15 minutes
COOKING TIME: 7¼ to 9¾ hours

RECIPE VARIATION
Campanelle is my favorite pasta to use for this dish, but elbow macaroni, farfalle, or conchiglie are also great with it. Fun pasta shapes go a long way to get picky eaters to try new sauces.

CAULIFREDO

★ SOY-FREE   ★ GLUTEN-FREE   ★ OIL-FREE

This alfredo-esque sauce has no oil but is still thick and rich. The cauliflower gives it a bit of a cheezy taste, and the herbs balance it all out for a healthy and elegant dinner.

2 cups (475 ml) water

2 cups (200 g) cauliflower florets

½ cup (108 g) dry white beans (any except cannellini)

1 teaspoon Italian Seasoning (page 22)

1 tablespoon (2.5 g) fresh basil or 1 teaspoon dried basil

½ teaspoon salt

Pepper, to taste

Add the water, cauliflower, beans, and Italian Seasoning to your slow cooker. Cook on low for 7 to 9 hours.

Carefully transfer the cooked mixture to a blender and add the basil and salt. Purée until smooth. Add pepper, taste, and adjust salt if needed.

YIELD: about 3 cups (700 ml)

PER 1-CUP SERVING: 126.7 calories; 0.5 g total fat; 0.1 g saturated fat; 9.3 g protein; 23.5 g carbohydrate; 10.0 g dietary fiber; 0 mg cholesterol

PREP TIME: 15 minutes

COOKING TIME: 7 to 9 hours

DID YOU KNOW?
Adding a mashed member of the cabbage family of vegetables, such as cauliflower or turnips, lends the sharpness that cheese provides in non-vegan fare. I like to add these vegetables to soups, fondues, and pasta to healthfully mimic that cheezy flavor without nutritional yeast.

ROOT VEGGIE BARLEY RISOTTO

★ SOY-FREE ★ OIL-FREE

Ever since I got a winter CSA, I've been in love with the humble turnip and greens of all kinds. You have to get creative when the same veggies get dropped on your doorstep every week. Using barley gives a much-needed change from the typical rice and allows this risotto to cook all day.

FOR THE MORNING INGREDIENTS:

2 cups (475 ml) water

½ cup (92 g) barley

½ cup (65 g) diced carrots

½ cup (75 g) diced turnips or rutabagas, peeled

½ cup (67 g) diced sweet potatoes or (70 g) winter squash

2 cloves garlic, minced

½ teaspoon dried oregano

½ teaspoon dried sage

FOR THE EVENING INGREDIENTS:

1 cup (56 g) minced greens (such as turnips, collards, kale, etc.)

½ teaspoon lemon zest

Salt and pepper, to taste

In the morning: Add all the morning ingredients to the slow cooker and cook on low for 7 to 9 hours.

Thirty minutes before serving: Add the greens and lemon zest. Right before serving, add salt and pepper to taste. Also add more oregano and/or sage if needed.

YIELD: about 3 cups (580 g)
PER 1-CUP SERVING: 158.8 calories; 0.8 g total fat; 0 g saturated fat; 4.4 g protein; 33.6 g carbohydrate; 7.1 g dietary fiber; 0 mg cholesterol
PREP TIME: 15 minutes
COOKING TIME: 7½ to 9½ hours

DID YOU KNOW?

What's the difference between turnips and rutabagas? Rutabagas are usually larger than turnips, have yellowish flesh that is a little starchier, and are less perfectly round than most turnips. If you're buying rutabagas in a grocery store, they are often waxed, but you will need to peel rutabagas whether they're waxed or not.

CORN AND BASIL RISOTTO

★ SOY-FREE   ★ GLUTEN-FREE   ★ OIL-FREE

This risotto cooks fast, and I like to make it for dinner on summer evenings. It cooks while you take a walk, work in the garden, or set up the deck for dinner. It includes the corn kernels, but it also utilizes the corncob to squeeze every last bit of flavor out of your fresh corn.

2 cups (475 g) water

½ cup (115 g) Arborio rice

1 medium ear of corn (about ½ cup [77 g] kernels), kernels removed and cob cut into 4 pieces

Three 2-inch (5 cm) sprigs thyme

2 tablespoons (5 g) chopped fresh basil

Salt and pepper, to taste

Extra chopped basil, for garnish

Add the water, rice, and corn kernels to the slow cooker. Press in the 4 cob pieces and fresh thyme. These last two ingredients are what make the broth really special.

Cook on high for about 1 hour. Check at 40 to 45 minutes in case your slow cooker cooks quicker. If the risotto is getting too dry, just add a bit of extra water.

Remove the corncob pieces and thyme stems. Stir in the basil and serve. Top with additional basil if you want to make it look extra-special.

YIELD: about 3 cups (615 g)
PER 1-CUP SERVING: 129.9 calories; 0 g total fat; 0 g saturated fat; 2.8 g protein; 29.4 g carbohydrate; 1.2 g dietary fiber; 0 mg cholesterol
PREP TIME: 15 minutes
COOKING TIME: 1 hour

RECIPE VARIATIONS
- Use short-grain brown rice in place of the Arborio to make this a whole-grain dish.
- No fresh corncobs? Add 2 teaspoons (5 g) of any vegan bouillon you have on hand instead or replace the water with vegetable broth. That way you can have it in the middle of winter, too!

MUSHROOM BARLEY RISOTTO

★ SOY-FREE OPTION*   ★ OIL-FREE OPTION**

I love these barley risottos because they can cook all day. This one is full of mushrooms, dill, and vegan sour cream or cashew cream. The Slavic cuisine flavors make it a great choice for a chilly or snowy day. As a bonus, it can be made with staples from your pantry and fridge; plus, it cooks while you are out playing in the snow.

FOR THE MORNING INGREDIENTS:

2 cups (475 g) water

1 cup (70 g) chopped mushrooms

½ cup (92 g) barley

½ cup (65 g) diced carrots

2 cloves garlic, minced

1 vegan bouillon cube

1 teaspoon dried dill

FOR THE EVENING INGREDIENTS:

½ cup (115 g) vegan sour cream, **Extra-Thick Silken Tofu Sour Cream (page 28), or *Cashew Cream (page 28)

Salt and pepper, to taste

Extra dill, for serving

In the morning: Add all the morning ingredients and cook on low for 7 to 9 hours.

Right before serving: Stir in the vegan sour cream (or substitute) and then add the salt and pepper to taste. Serve with extra dill.

YIELD: about 3 cups (580 g)
PER 1-CUP SERVING: 251.2 calories; 11.2 g total fat; 4.8 g saturated fat; 6.9 g protein; 32.7 g carbohydrate; 8.7 g dietary fiber; 0 mg cholesterol
PREP TIME: 15 minutes
COOKING TIME: 7 to 9 hours

NO-MORE-BOTTLED PASTA SAUCE

★ SOY-FREE ★ GLUTEN-FREE ★ OIL-FREE

There's no need to buy pasta sauce at the store when it's this easy to make.
Just package the leftovers in the amount that works for one meal for you or your family
and freeze it. You can also create any variation you want.

1 can (28 ounces, or 800 g) crushed tomatoes or 3 cups (540 g) fresh tomatoes, puréed

1 cup (70 g) minced mushrooms

¼ cup (60 ml) red wine or 2 tablespoons (28 ml) balsamic vinegar

4 cloves garlic

1 tablespoon (13 g) sugar or ¼ teaspoon stevia

2 teaspoons (3 g) Italian Seasoning (page 22)

1 teaspoon oregano

Salt and pepper, to taste

Add all the ingredients except for the salt and pepper to your slow cooker and cook on low for 7 to 9 hours. Then add the salt and pepper until it tastes just the way you like it.

YIELD: about 4 cups (950 ml)
PER 1-CUP (235 ML) SERVING: 77.3 calories; 0.1 g total fat; 0 g saturated fat; 0.7 g protein; 15.6 g carbohydrate; 7.3 g dietary fiber; 0 mg cholesterol
PREP TIME: 15 minutes
COOKING TIME: 7 to 9 hours

RECIPE VARIATIONS

- The variations are endless with this recipe. Try using onions and peppers in place of the mushrooms.
- Green olives, kalamata olives, eggplant, summer squash, winter squash, or turnips can all be rotated through to keep your sauce new and exciting.

CHAPTER NINE

VEGAN SQUARES:
FULL MEALS LAYERED IN THE SLOW COOKER

IN SOME WAYS, this is the most exciting chapter in the whole book. I've been working on self-contained meals from the slow cooker for a while, and I finally feel like they are ready to share with you.

Some of these are layered right in the slow cooker, and others have one or more of the layers packaged up in parchment paper to keep the flavors separate. But no matter which one you pick, you'll feel like you've had a proper square meal. Granted, you may still want to have some steamed rice or a nice wholesome chunk of bread on the side, but you will still end up with something very different than the typical stew or soup you may be used to making in your slow cooker.

Many of these recipes feature tofu, tempeh, and seitan, and if you're not fond of one of them, feel free to substitute the one you like more. You can even cook your favorite bean or veggie patty wrapped in a parchment package so all the moisture doesn't break it up.

These recipes serve two as is, but add rice, bread, and/or a big salad and they'll stretch to serve three just fine.

TOFU BRAISED WITH PEARS AND BRUSSELS SPROUTS

★ GLUTEN-FREE   ★ OIL-FREE OPTION*

Cheryl, my picky eater, hated brussels sprouts until I cooked them with maple syrup and pecans. I built on that in this dish and used pear and agave for sweetness, kept the pecans, and threw in some liquid smoke and port wine to give it a rich, grown-up flavor. You'll love to this colorful dinner.

FOR THE SAUCE:

¾ cup (175 ml) water

¼ cup (60 ml) port wine

¼ teaspoon liquid smoke

1 tablespoon (20 g) agave nectar

Pinch each salt and pepper

8 ounces (225 g) tofu, pressed and cut into 4 pieces

1½ cups (132 g) shredded brussels sprouts

1½ cups (165 g) shredded carrot

1 cup (161 g) chopped pear

¼ cup (28 g) chopped pecans

Oil your slow cooker with a little spray oil or *line with parchment paper to make recipe oil-free. Mix the sauce ingredients in your slow cooker and immerse the tofu as much as possible. Top with the brussels sprouts and carrots and then add the pear and pecans. Cook on low for 7 to 9 hours.

Mix together, taste, and add extra salt and pepper if needed. Serve with a piece of crusty bread.

YIELD: 2 servings

PER SERVING: 355.4 calories; 19.5 g total fat; 2.2 g saturated fat; 19.8 g protein; 37.2 g carbohydrate; 10.9 g dietary fiber; 0 mg cholesterol

PREP TIME: 20 minutes

COOKING TIME: 7 to 9 hours

RECIPE VARIATIONS

- Take this from a one-pot dinner to a layered dinner by wrapping the veggies in a piece of parchment paper and the pear and pecans in another. Of course, you can still pour the sauce on everything.
- Try this recipe if you think you aren't a brussels sprout fan. A little sweetness from the pears mixed with the almost smoky flavor of the pecans really mellows them out.

ITALIAN SEITAN COINS WITH MASHED CAULIFLOWER AND GRAVY

★ SOY-FREE   ★ OIL-FREE OPTION*

Seitan cooked with mushrooms forms the base of the gravy, and you can't go wrong with mashed cauliflower or cute baby carrots. To keep the flavors from melding like a stew, the carrot layer and the cauliflower layer are cooked in parchment packets. Tear a bigger piece of parchment than you think you'll use so it will overlap. Lay it out on a cutting board and put the ingredient(s) in the middle. Bring together two of the sides of the paper and fold over two times. Then take the other ends, pull them down, and tuck them under. Carefully place the packet in the slow cooker.

FOR THE SEITAN LAYER:

1 cup (130 g) Italian Seitan Coins (page 16) or store-bought vegan Italian sausage, sliced

1 cup (235 ml) water

½ cup (35 g) minced mushrooms

1 tablespoon (8 g) flour

Salt and pepper, to taste

FOR THE CAULIFLOWER LAYER:

2 cups (200 g) cauliflower florets

1 whole clove garlic, optional

¼ cup (60 ml) unsweetened nondairy milk

Salt and pepper, to taste

FOR THE CARROT LAYER:

1½ cups (195 g) baby carrots or regular carrots cut into coins

Oil your slow cooker with a little spray oil or *line with parchment to make cleanup easier and make the recipe oil-free. Add the Italian Seitan Coins, water, and mushrooms (you'll add the flour, salt, and pepper later).

Place the cauliflower and garlic, if using, in a piece of parchment paper. Close and place on top of the seitan mixture. Then put the carrots in another piece of parchment and close. Place on top. Cook on low for 7 to 9 hours.

Before serving: Remove the parchment bundles and set aside. Whisk the flour into the seitan layer to make a gravy. Add additional water if needed. Add salt and pepper to taste.

In a food processor, add the cooked cauliflower, garlic, if using, and nondairy milk and purée. Add salt and pepper to taste.

Serve your three-course meal and know that you have only one slow cooker to clean up! You can serve it dressed up with the seitan on a bed of the mashed cauliflower, gravy ladled over both and a pile of carrots on the side. No matter how you serve it, there should be enough gravy to put on your seitan and your mash.

YIELD: 2 servings
PER SERVING: 240.6 calories; 2.4 g total fat; 0.3 g saturated fat; 26.9 g protein; 31.1 g carbohydrate; 7.7 g dietary fiber; 0 mg cholesterol
PREP TIME: 15 minutes
COOKING TIME: 7 to 9 hours

RECIPE VARIATION
Make a gluten- and soy-free version by using 1 can (15 ounces, or 425 g) chickpeas (1½ cups, or 360 g) plus 1 teaspoon of the Italian Seasoning instead of seitan.

BEAN AND OAT VEGGIE CHILI OVER BAKED SWEET POTATO

★ SOY-FREE ★ GLUTEN-FREE ★ OIL-FREE

Sweet potatoes are a powerhouse of vitamin A, and oat groats have all the goodness of oats with the bonus of digesting slowly, which keeps you feeling full longer. That makes this an easy, nutritious, and inexpensive meal.

FOR THE MORNING INGREDIENTS:

1 medium sweet potato, unpeeled if organic

2 cups (475 ml) water

½ cup (97 g) dry Vaquero or pinto beans

¼ cup (46 g) oat groats (Make sure they are clearly marked gluten-free.)

¼ cup (33 g) diced carrot

¼ cup (38 g) diced bell pepper

2 cloves garlic, minced

½ teaspoon oregano

½ teaspoon chipotle powder

¼ teaspoon turmeric

FOR THE EVENING INGREDIENTS:

1 cup (56 g) chopped greens

2 tablespoons (32 g) tomato paste

Salt and pepper, to taste

In the morning: Take the sweet potato and poke holes in it with a fork and set aside. Add all the other morning ingredients to your slow cooker. Place the sweet potato on top of the mixture. It will sink into the chili, which is fine. Cook on low for 7 to 9 hours.

About 20 minutes before serving: Remove the sweet potato and set on a plate. Turn the slow cooker to high. Mix the chili and add a bit more water if it's too dry. Now stir in the greens and tomato paste. Pop the sweet potato back in to keep it hot. Cook for about 20 minutes or until the greens are cooked the way you like them.

Carefully remove the hot sweet potato with tongs, cut it in half, and put each half in its own bowl. Taste the chili and add salt and pepper to suit your taste. Smother each sweet potato half with chili and serve.

YIELD: 2 servings
PER SERVING: 253.2 calories; 2.3 g total fat; 0.4 g saturated fat; 11.1 g protein; 50.4 g carbohydrate; 10.7 g dietary fiber; 0 mg cholesterol
PREP TIME: 15 minutes
COOKING TIME: 7½ to 9½ hours

RECIPE VARIATIONS
- Serve with any of your favorite chili toppings such as vegan sour cream, vegan cheese, hot sauce, etc.
- Instead of waiting 20 minutes for the greens and tomato paste to cook, just stir them in and serve. The greens will still cook a bit from the heat of the stew, and if you cut them smaller, the texture will be pretty much the same.
- This recipe calls for oat groats, but if you don't have any, feel free to substitute steel-cut oats.

ALL-IN-ONE THANKSGIVING DINNER

★ OIL-FREE ★ SOY-FREE OPTION* ★ GLUTEN-FREE OPTION**

You may not want to go through all of the trouble of making a big holiday meal if you're cooking for only one or two. This three-layered dinner takes no time to put together and is a complete Thanksgiving dinner. All that's missing is the pumpkin pie!

FOR THE BOTTOM LAYER (TEMPEH AND GRAVY):

1 cup (235 ml) water

2 tablespoons (14 g) Golden Veggie Bouillon Powder (page 26)

Pinch each salt and pepper

8 ounces (225 g) tempeh (*or seitan for soy-free), cut into 2 slices

1 to 2 tablespoons (8 to 16 g) flour (**or gluten-free thickener)

FOR THE MIDDLE LAYER (STUFFING):

1½ cups (42 g) packaged vegan stuffing (**or gluten-free stuffing)

½ cup (120 ml) water

¼ cup (28 g) minced cranberries or pecans

FOR THE TOP LAYER (CANDIED SWEET POTATOES):

1 medium sweet potato, cut into thick rounds

1 tablespoon (15 g) brown sugar

¼ teaspoon cinnamon

Pinch salt

Tear off 2 pieces of parchment paper or aluminum foil big enough to make an enclosed packet in the slow cooker. You will use these for the middle and top layers. Set aside.

Add the water, Golden Veggie Bouillon Powder, salt, and pepper to the slow cooker and mix. Add the tempeh (or seitan). Set the flour aside for use right before serving.

In a bowl, mix the stuffing ingredients. Transfer the mixture to the middle of one of the pieces of parchment and close it up so it will fit in the slow cooker. Place on top of the tempeh.

Spread out the other piece of parchment and arrange the sweet potato slices on it and sprinkle with sugar, cinnamon, and salt. You may need to stack them so they will fit in the slow cooker: close up this package, place it on top of the stuffing packet, and replace the lid.

Cook on low for 7 to 9 hours (or 3 hours on high). Remove the top two packets and set aside. Turn the slow cooker to high, remove the tempeh, and set aside. Whisk in the flour and set the tempeh back in. The gravy should thicken up enough while you plate up the potatoes and stuffing. Add a little more flour if needed. Place the tempeh on the plates and cover with gravy and stuffing.

YIELD: 2 servings
PER SERVING: 584.4 calories; 14.2 g total fat; 1.9 g saturated fat; 17.2 g protein; 93.5 g carbohydrate; 2.7 g dietary fiber; 0 mg cholesterol
PREP TIME: 20 minutes
COOKING TIME: 7 to 9 hours on low or 3 hours on high

ROASTED VEGGIES AND TEMPEH (OR SEITAN OR BEANS . . .)

★ GLUTEN-FREE OPTION* ★ OIL-FREE ★ SOY-FREE OPTION**

This is a great way to use up those winter root vegetables. Feel free to mix and match depending on what you have on hand. This meal is even better with some steamed green veggies or a big salad, but it will still fill you up all by itself.

FOR THE TEMPEH MARINADE:

½ teaspoon soy sauce (*use gluten-free or ** coconut amino for soy-free)

½ teaspoon balsamic vinegar

Few drops liquid smoke

1 cup (166 g) diced tempeh, or (270 g) seitan (*for soy-free), or (160 g) precooked beans (*for soy-free)

½ cup (68 g) diced peeled beets

½ cup (55 g) diced potatoes (Purple are beautiful in this dish.)

½ cup (75 g) diced peeled turnip, radish, or peeled rutabaga

½ cup (65 g) diced carrots or (70 g) winter squash

¼ cup (39 g) diced celeriac or (25 g) celery

½ teaspoon minced garlic

One 2-inch (5 cm) sprig fresh rosemary

¼ cup (60 ml) water

Mix the marinade ingredients together and toss in the tempeh. You can do this right before cooking or earlier and let it marinate in the fridge for 2 to 8 hours. Add all the ingredients to your slow cooker and cook on low for 7 to 9 hours.

YIELD: 2 servings
PER SERVING: 232.1 calories; 9.2 g total fat; 1.9 g saturated fat; 17.6 g protein; 24.0 g carbohydrate; 3.5 g dietary fiber; 0 mg cholesterol
PREP TIME: 20 minutes
COOKING TIME: 7 to 9 hours

DID YOU KNOW?
Radishes change into something amazing once they are roasted in the slow cooker or the oven. They are juicy and lose that spicy bite to fit into almost any dish.

TEMPEH WITH APPLES AND CABBAGE

★ GLUTEN-FREE   ★ OIL-FREE OPTION*

This dish gets its sweetness from the apples and maple syrup and a little tartness from the apple cider vinegar. Add cabbage, onions, and tempeh, and you have a one-dish dinner that's not the same old thing!

2 cups (140 g) shredded cabbage

1 cup (125 g) peeled and chopped apple

½ cup (120 ml) water

1 bouillon cube

1 teaspoon apple cider vinegar

1 teaspoon maple syrup

2 cloves garlic, minced

Pinch each salt and pepper

8 ounces (225 g) tempeh, cut into slices

½ small onion, sliced thin

1 teaspoon caraway seeds

Oil your slow cooker with a little spray oil or *line with parchment to make cleanup easier and make the recipe oil-free. Add the cabbage, apple, and water to your slow cooker. Mix in the bouillon cube, vinegar, maple syrup, garlic, salt, and pepper.

Layer the tempeh on the cabbage mixture and top the tempeh with the onions and caraway. You can add another pinch of salt and pepper at this point, but you can also let people add that at the table themselves.

Cook on low for 7 to 9 hours.

YIELD: 2 servings
PER SERVING: 302.4 calories; 8.3 g total fat; 1.1 g saturated fat; 11.8 g protein; 23.2 g carbohydrate; 3.2 g dietary fiber; 0 mg cholesterol
PREP TIME: 20 minutes
COOKING TIME: 7 to 9 hours

RECIPE VARIATION

If you're not a fan of tempeh and don't want to add seitan, instead try using 1½ cups (246 g) cooked chickpeas (or one 15 ounce, [425 g] can).

INDIAN STUFFED EGGPLANT AND TEMPEH TANDOORI

★ GLUTEN-FREE OPTION* ★ OIL-FREE OPTION** ★ SOY-FREE OPTION***

No need to go out for an expensive Indian meal when you can make a fancy two-course meal at home. All you need to go with it is some steamed brown basmati rice, so use the timer on your rice cooker if you have one to coordinate your dinner.

FOR THE EGGPLANT LAYER:

¼ cup (20 g) shredded coconut

⅛ cup (18 g) peanuts

1 tablespoon (8 g) grated ginger

1½ teaspoons (7.5 g) tamarind paste

½ teaspoon Garam Masala (page 21)

¼ teaspoon turmeric

¼ teaspoon coriander

⅛ teaspoon chili powder

2 cloves garlic, minced

3 to 4 egg-sized mini eggplant

½ cup (120 ml) water

FOR THE TANDOORI LAYER:

¼ cup (60 g) unsweetened vegan yogurt (**use coconut yogurt for soy-free)

2 cloves garlic, minced

1 teaspoon paprika

½ teaspoon each Garam Masala (page 21), turmeric, and grated ginger

Pinch salt

8 ounces (225 g) tempeh, cut into 8 slices (***use seitan for soy-free)

Oil your slow cooker with a little spray oil or **line with parchment to make cleanup easier and make the recipe oil-free.

In a food processor add the coconut through the garlic and purée. Add a tablespoon (15 ml) of water if the mixture is too thick to purée. It won't be smooth but will be a rough paste.

Cut the eggplant in half, stopping just before they split in two so the pieces are still connected by the stem end. Cut again to split it into quarters that are still connected. Stuff the eggplants with the curry paste you just made.

All the paste won't fit into the eggplants, so mix the leftover curry paste and water in the bottom of the slow cooker. Then carefully place the eggplants in.

Mix the yogurt through the salt in a bowl. Take a piece of parchment paper or aluminum foil and spread on about ⅓ of the yogurt sauce. Then layer the tempeh (or seitan) in and cover with the rest of the sauce. Close up the parchment (or foil) and place on top of the eggplant. Cook on low for Serve over steamed brown basmati rice or with a piece of roti, an Indian flatbread (*use gluten-free).

YIELD: 2 servings

PER SERVING: 402.4 calories; 15.1 g total fat; 5.0 g saturated fat; 20.0 g protein; 57.1 g carbohydrate; 19.7 g dietary fiber; 0 mg cholesterol

PREP TIME: 15 minutes

COOKING TIME: 7 to 9 hours

RECIPE VARIATION

Fancy up your meal by making a biryani, an Indian rice pilaf. All you have to do is add some whole cloves, black cardamom pods, and a cinnamon stick in the rice pot or steamer when you begin to cook your rice.

BLACK PEPPER PORTOBELLO AND BAKED POTATO DINNER

★ SOY-FREE ★ GLUTEN-FREE ★ OIL-FREE OPTION*

This is a traditional square meal similar to the one I grew up on. This version, however, is 100 percent plant-based, unlike the meals my momma made.

2 to 3 large portobello mushrooms

Few pinches each salt and pepper

FOR THE SAUCE:

½ cup (120 ml) water

1 tablespoon (16 g) tomato paste

2 teaspoons (10 g) brown sugar or agave nectar

1 teaspoon balsamic vinegar

½ teaspoon tamarind paste

½ teaspoon vegan Worcestershire sauce

2 medium baking potatoes

2 cups (264 g) mixed broccoli, cauliflower, and carrots (fresh or frozen thawed in the fridge)

Oil the slow cooker or *line with parchment paper to make the recipe oil-free. Rinse the mushrooms and remove the stems. (You can use them in another dish.) Salt and pepper both sides of the mushrooms. Layer them in the bottom of the slow cooker.

Mix the sauce ingredients together and then pour over the mushrooms. Wash the potatoes and poke holes in them. Place them on top of the mushrooms and cook on low for 7 to 9 hours.

Thirty to 45 minutes before serving: Turn the slow cooker to high and put in the remaining veggies. Cook for 30 to 45 minutes or until tender and heated through.

YIELD: 2 servings
PER SERVING: 278.9 calories; 0.9 g total fat; 0.2 g saturated fat; 9.2 g protein; 63.9 g carbohydrate; 10.3 g dietary fiber; 0 mg cholesterol
PREP TIME: 10 minutes
COOKING TIME: 7½ to 9¾ hours

RECIPE VARIATION
If you are a huge fan of pepper like I am, add extra and press it into the wet mushroom with your hand. I love the surprise burst of heat every now and again.

ETHIOPIAN STYLE TEMPEH W'ET AND VEGGIE MEAL

★ SOY-FREE OPTION* ★ GLUTEN-FREE ★ OIL-FREE OPTION**

The spice mix in this recipe is called berbere and is spicy. However, you can make your own from the Berbere Spice Mix (page 22) and tone the heat down. The veggies are in a mild blend of turmeric and cumin to balance out your meal. *W'et* is the Ethiopian word for stew.

FOR THE TEMPEH LAYER:

1½ cups (355 ml) water

1 tablespoon (5.5 g) cooked onion (page 19)

1 tablespoon (8 g) grated ginger

2 cloves garlic, minced

2 teaspoons (10 ml) red wine or balsamic vinegar

1 to 2 teaspoons (2.3 to 4.6 g) Berbere Spice Mix (page 22), to taste

1 teaspoon Golden Veggie Bouillon Powder (page 26) or ½ bouillon cube

1 teaspoon paprika

½ teaspoon lemon juice

¼ teaspoon cardamom

Pinch salt

8 ounces (225 g) tempeh, cut into cubes (*use seitan for soy-free)

FOR THE VEGGIE LAYER:

1 cup (70 g) shredded cabbage

1 cup (110 g) chopped potato

1 medium carrot, cut into thick coins

1 clove garlic, minced

1 teaspoon olive oil (**omit for oil-free)

1 teaspoon turmeric

¼ teaspoon cumin

Pinch each salt and pepper

Oil your slow cooker with a little spray oil or **line with parchment to make cleanup easier and make the recipe oil-free.

For the tempeh layer, mix the water through the salt in your slow cooker and then add in the tempeh and stir to coat.

Mix all the veggie layer ingredients together in a bowl. Next, take a piece of parchment paper and pile in the veggie mixture and close. Carefully place this on top of the tempeh mixture. Cook on low for 7 to 9 hours.

YIELD: 2 servings
PER SERVING: 342.9 calories; 10.5 g total fat; 1.3 g saturated fat; 24.7 g protein; 31.8 g carbohydrate; 15.6 g dietary fiber; 0 mg cholesterol
PREP TIME: 15 minutes
COOKING TIME: 7 to 9 hours

DID YOU KNOW?

Ethiopian food is usually served with a wonderful sourdough flatbread called *injera* that's made of ground teff, which is a gluten-free grain. It's out of scope of this book, but you can find recipes online or grab some at your local Ethiopian restaurant. If you're gluten-free, be sure to tell them because they sometimes mix in regular flour.

MUSHROOM TEMPEH OVER POTATOES AND CARROTS

★ GLUTEN-FREE   ★ SOY-FREE OPTION*   ★ OIL-FREE OPTION**

The mushrooms release their juices during cooking, infusing the tempeh with a rich flavor while the carrots and the onions season the potatoes. This meal has all the taste of a long-cooking stew, but you end up with a plate of three separate dishes!

FOR THE POTATO LAYER:

3 cups (330 g) sliced potatoes

1 tablespoon (15 ml) olive oil
(**omit for oil-free)

½ teaspoon dried thyme

¼ teaspoon ground rosemary or
½ teaspoon dried rosemary

Pinch each salt and pepper

FOR THE CARROT LAYER:

1 large carrot, cut into thick coins

FOR THE TEMPEH LAYER:

8 ounces (225 g) tempeh, cut in
quarters (*use seitan for soy-free)

½ cup (35 g) chopped mushrooms

¾ cup (175 ml) water

Spray the crock to make cleanup easier or **line with parchment paper to make the recipe oil-free.

Toss potatoes with the olive oil (if using), herbs, salt, and pepper. Layer the coated potatoes in the bottom of the slow cooker.

Add carrot coins next, then tempeh pieces, and top with mushrooms. Pour the water over the top of everything. Cook on low for 7 to 9 hours.

YIELD: 2 servings
PER SERVING: 366 calories; 14.9 g total fat; 1.9 g saturated fat; 24.4 g protein; 33.1 g carbohydrate; 2.9 g dietary fiber; 0 mg cholesterol
PREP TIME: 15 minutes
COOKING TIME: 7 to 9 hours

RECIPE VARIATION

If you find yourself low on carrots, go ahead and use other root veggies you might have on hand, such as parsnips, radishes, sweet potato, or celeriac.

CHAPTER TEN

SWEET TREATS:
DRINKS, SYRUPS, AND DESSERTS

THIS CHAPTER FEATURES my new favorite recipe for stirring into iced coffee, pouring over ice cream, and folding into warm breakfast grains—Pumpkin Coconut Caramel Sauce (page x). In addition, there are a couple of cocoas that are special enough to double as dessert all by themselves.

I love using my small slow cooker to make mini cakes or even an after-dinner cookie. These are my slow cooker versions of all those microwavable treats for one. I don't like the texture that microwaving produces in baked goods. Slow-cooked baked goods, on the other hand, are super-moist and develop a firm texture on the outside part that touches the crock. They don't cook in 5 minutes, but if you start them right before you eat, they will be ready when you are!

CHOCOLATE CHIP COOKIE FOR TWO (WITH TONS OF VARIATIONS)

★ SOY-FREE ★ GLUTEN-FREE OPTION* ★ OIL-FREE OPTION**

No matter how many people you're feeding, eventually you'll want a sweet treat. This recipe makes a warm, ooey gooey cookie for two. Use your favorite nuts or extracts to change it up. You could make variations on this recipe to have a different cookie every night!

FOR THE DRY INGREDIENTS:

½ cup (60 g) whole-wheat pastry flour (*use gluten-free baking mix)

1 tablespoon (15 g) brown sugar

⅛ teaspoon baking soda

Pinch salt

FOR THE WET INGREDIENTS:

¼ cup (60 ml) unsweetened nondairy milk

1 teaspoon ground flaxseeds mixed with 2 teaspoons (10 ml) warm water

1 teaspoon olive oil (**substitute applesauce or pumpkin purée)

¼ teaspoon extract (vanilla, orange, lemon, mint, lavender, etc.)

EXTRAS:

¼ cup (44 g) vegan chocolate chips or

¼ cup (44 g) vegan chocolate chips and ¼ cup (30 g) chopped nuts or

½ cup (60 g) chopped nuts

Spray the crock with oil or **line with parchment paper to make the recipe oil-free.

Mix the dry ingredients in one bowl and the wet ingredients in another. Then add the wet to the dry and mix until combined. Add in the extras of your choice.

Pour the mixture into the slow cooker and spread evenly on the bottom. Put a clean dish towel or paper towel between the lid and slow cooker to absorb the condensation.

Cook on high for 45 to 60 minutes or until the middle springs back when touched.

YIELD: 2 servings
PER SERVING (USING ¼ CUP [44 G] CHOCOLATE CHIPS AND ¼ CUP [30 G] NUTS): 470.4 calories; 29.3 g total fat; 3.8 g saturated fat; 5.5 g protein; 49.5 g carbohydrate; 8.5 g dietary fiber; 0 mg cholesterol
PREP TIME: 15 minutes
COOKING TIME: 45 to 60 minutes

RECIPE VARIATION

Try one of these combinations:

• Vanilla extract, walnuts, and vegan chocolate chips

• Lemon extract and almonds with or without vegan chocolate chips

• Mint extract and vegan chocolate chips

• Lavender extract and vegan chocolate chips

CHAI-SPICED APPLE CRUMBLE

★ SOY-FREE   ★ OIL-FREE   ★ GLUTEN-FREE OPTION*

This crumble is full of juicy apples and pecans as well as a spice blend based on my favorite chai tea. The topping of rolled oats and whole-wheat flour is packed with even more spices, making this a bold crumble your family will love!

FOR THE FILLING:

2 cups (300 g) chopped apple

¼ cup (28 g) minced pecans

⅛ cup (30 g) packed brown sugar

¼ teaspoon each ground cardamom and cinnamon

⅛ teaspoon each ground ginger and nutmeg

Pinch each allspice and cloves

FOR THE TOPPING:

¼ cup (20 g) rolled oats

⅛ cup (15 g) whole-wheat pastry flour (*use gluten-free baking mix)

⅛ cup (30 g) packed brown sugar

1 tablespoon (15 ml) nondairy milk

⅛ teaspoon each ground cardamom and cinnamon

1⁄16 teaspoon each ground ginger and nutmeg

Pinch each ground allspice and cloves

Mix all the filling ingredients in the slow cooker. Mix the topping ingredients in a separate bowl and drop by teaspoons on top of the filling.

Cook on high for 1 hour. You can pour some coconut creamer over the top or pair with vegan vanilla ice cream if you want to be decadent.

YIELD: 4 servings
PER SERVING: 173.5 calories; 6.0 g total fat; 0.6 g saturated fat; 1.9 g protein; 35.3 g carbohydrate; 3.4 g dietary fiber; 0 mg cholesterol
PREP TIME: 15 minutes
COOKING TIME: 1 hour

RECIPE VARIATION
Branch out and make berry, peach, or apricot crumbles. You can use any in-season fruit—even frozen fruit will work in this recipe.

OATMEAL AND DRIED FRUIT COOKIE FOR TWO

★ SOY-FREE   ★ GLUTEN-FREE OPTION*   ★ OIL-FREE OPTION**

I've been fascinated with the recent trend of microwaving desserts in mugs. But I hate the texture that a microwave gives food, especially sweets. So this is my slow cooker cookie version for two. Just pour the batter in right before you eat, and dessert will be hot and waiting when you're done.

FOR THE DRY INGREDIENTS:

¼ cup (30 g) whole-wheat pastry flour (*use gluten-free baking mix)

¼ cup (20 g) rolled oats

¼ teaspoon stevia or 1 tablespoon (20 g) agave nectar

¼ teaspoon cinnamon

⅛ teaspoon baking soda

Pinch salt

FOR THE WET INGREDIENTS:

¼ cup (60 ml) unsweetened nondairy milk

1 teaspoon ground flaxseeds mixed with 2 teaspoons (10 ml) warm water

1 teaspoon olive oil (**substitute applesauce or pumpkin purée)

¼ teaspoon vanilla extract

EXTRAS:

¼ cup (30 g) dried cranberries or

¼ cup (35 g) raisins or

¼ cup (35 g) any minced dried fruit

Spray the crock with oil or **line with parchment paper to make the recipe oil-free.

Mix the dry ingredients in one bowl and the wet ingredients in another. Then add the wet to the dry and mix until combined. Add in the dried fruit of your choice.

Pour the mixture into the slow cooker and spread evenly on the bottom. Put a clean dish towel or paper towel between the lid and slow cooker to absorb the condensation.

Cook on high for 45 to 60 minutes or until the middle springs back when touched.

YIELD: 2 servings
PER SERVING: 240.2 calories; 4.3 g total fat; 0.5 g saturated fat; 4.1 g protein; 47.6 g carbohydrate; 5.2 g dietary fiber; 0 mg cholesterol
PREP TIME: 15 minutes
COOKING TIME: 45 to 60 minutes

RECIPE VARIATION

Try this with a big scoop of vanilla nondairy ice cream and maybe a drizzle of one of the syrup or caramel recipes in this book for a dessert no one will ever forget.

APPLE CHOCOLATE CHIP NUT BREAD PUDDING

★ SOY-FREE ★ GLUTEN-FREE OPTION* ★ OIL-FREE OPTION**

This is the perfect end to a dinner party and the leftovers heat up great if it's just for you. Bread pudding is never going to win a beauty contest, but this one is moist and flecked with nuts and chocolate. The apple brandy adds to the complex flavor of this delicious dessert.

2 cups (60 g) stale whole-wheat bread (*use gluten-free)

1½ cups (225 g) peeled minced apple

½ to 1 cup (120 to 235 ml) nondairy milk, as needed

2 tablespoons (28 ml) apple brandy, optional

1 tablespoon (7 g) ground flaxseeds mixed with 2 tablespoons (28 ml) warm water

¼ cup (50 g) sugar or ½ teaspoon stevia (or sweetener of your choice, to taste)

⅓ cup (40 g) chopped nuts (walnuts, pecans, etc.)

¼ cup (44 g) minced vegan chocolate chips

Oil your slow cooker crock or **line with parchment paper to make recipe oil-free. Soak the bread in a large bowl with the apples, ½ cup (120 ml) of the milk, apple brandy, flaxseed mixture, and sweetener for about 10 minutes. Add up to ½ cup (120 ml) more nondairy milk if the mixture is too dry.

Mix in the nuts and chocolate and then scrape the entire mixture into the slow cooker. Cook on high for 1½ to 2 hours.

YIELD: 4 servings
PER SERVING (WITH NUTS): 400.2 calories; 12.7 g total fat; 2.4 g saturated fat; 8.8 g protein; 60.6 g carbohydrate; 7.8 g dietary fiber; 0 mg cholesterol
PREP TIME: 15 minutes
COOKING TIME: 1½ to 2 hours

RECIPE VARIATION
This recipe, like some of the others in this chapter, begs for seasonal fruit. Try a berry bread pudding or peach and pecan with a little bourbon; the list goes on and on.

BLUEBERRY LEMON CAKE

★ SOY-FREE ★ GLUTEN-FREE OPTION* ★ OIL-FREE OPTION**

When you bake a cake like this one in your slow cooker, it becomes moist and sumptuous.
But you don't want the condensation making it wet and preventing it from baking, so use
a clean dish towel under the lid to soak up the moisture. Just make sure to fold
the towel in quarters so it doesn't touch the hot sides of your slow cooker.

FOR THE DRY INGREDIENTS:

½ cup (60 g) whole-wheat pastry flour (*use gluten-free baking mix)

¼ teaspoon stevia plus 1 teaspoon agave nectar or sweetener of your choice, to taste

¼ teaspoon baking powder

FOR THE WET INGREDIENTS:

⅓ cup (80 ml) unsweetened nondairy milk

¼ cup (36 g) blueberries

1 teaspoon ground flaxseeds mixed with 2 teaspoons (10 ml) warm water

1 teaspoon olive oil (**substitute applesauce or pumpkin purée)

½ teaspoon lemon zest

¼ teaspoon vanilla extract

¼ teaspoon lemon extract

Spray the crock with oil or **line with parchment paper to make the recipe oil-free. Mix the dry ingredients in one bowl and the wet ingredients in another. Then add the wet to the dry and mix until combined.

Pour the mixture into the slow cooker and spread evenly on the bottom. Put a clean dish towel or paper towel between the lid and slow cooker to absorb the condensation.

Cook on high 60 to 80 minutes or until the middle is solid and doesn't indent when you touch it.

YIELD: 4 servings
PER SERVING: 79.0 calories; 2.2 g total fat; 0.2 g saturated fat; 2.3 g protein; 13.3 g carbohydrate; 2.4 g dietary fiber; 0 mg cholesterol
PREP TIME: 15 minutes
COOKING TIME: 60 to 80 minutes

RECIPE VARIATION

I love the flavors of lemon and blueberry together, though a mix of lemon and chocolate is really worth trying, too. Use ⅛ to ¼ cup (22 to 44 g) vegan chocolate chips in place of the blueberries for a much richer treat.

BUTTERSCOTCH RUM SAUCE

★ SOY-FREE   ★ GLUTEN-FREE   ★ OIL-FREE OPTION*

Use this sweet sauce with a hint of rum in your coffee, over vanilla vegan ice cream, or in a big steaming cup of hot chocolate. Yum!

1 can (13.5 ounces, or 400 ml) full-fat coconut milk

1 cup (225 g) packed brown sugar

2 teaspoons (10 ml) dark rum

1 teaspoon vanilla

1 to 2 tablespoons (14 to 28 g) vegan butter, to taste (*omit for oil-free)

Add all the ingredients except the vegan butter to your slow cooker and cook on low for 7 to 9 hours.

If using, melt the vegan butter and add. Pour into a container to cool and stir a few times as it cools to keep it better incorporated. Once cool, store in the fridge for up to 2 weeks.

YIELD: about 2½ cups (570 ml)
PER 2-TABLESPOON (28 ML) SERVING: 67.7 calories; 1.5 g total fat; 0.9 g saturated fat; 0.1 g protein; 18.5 g carbohydrate; 0 g dietary fiber; 0 mg cholesterol
PREP TIME: 15 minutes
COOKING TIME: 7 to 9 hours

RECIPE VARIATION
Please note that the sauce will separate when refrigerated, but just give it a good mix before you use it next. You can also heat it up in the microwave or on the stove.

PUMPKIN COCONUT CARAMEL SAUCE

★ SOY-FREE ★ GLUTEN-FREE ★ OIL-FREE

This rich, gooey sauce embodies fall. It's lightly spiced and perfect in a cup of coffee. But don't limit yourself—try it on vegan ice cream, dip cookies into it, or stir a bit into your morning oatmeal.

1 can (13.5 ounces, or 400 ml) full-fat coconut milk

1 cup (225 g) packed brown sugar

1 cup (245 g) pumpkin purée

½ teaspoon ground cinnamon

⅛ teaspoon ground cardamom

⅛ teaspoon ground allspice

Pinch cloves

Add all the ingredients to your slow cooker and cook on low for 7 to 9 hours. Store in the fridge and use a few teaspoons (15 to 20 ml) in your hot or iced coffee.

YIELD: about 3 cups (700 ml)

PER 2-TABLESPOON (28 ML) SERVING: 42.9 calories; 0.5 g total fat; 0.4 g saturated fat; 0.2 g protein; 13.1 g carbohydrate; 0.4 g dietary fiber; 0 mg cholesterol

PREP TIME: 15 minutes

COOKING TIME: 7 to 9 hours

RECIPE VARIATION

Whatever you do, make sure to add some of this sauce to your coffee. It's amazing in hot and iced coffees and is more than worth the effort! It's like drinking pumpkin pie and is way better than that name-brand coffee chain's pumpkin spice syrup, which isn't vegan anyway.

SMALL BATCH OF BASIC BROWNIES

★ SOY-FREE ★ GLUTEN-FREE OPTION* ★ OIL-FREE OPTION**

Sometimes all you need is a brownie. This recipe is for a plain super-moist brownie that's not overly sweet and loaded with flax and whole grains to offset the sugar a bit. Feel free to throw in some nuts, vegan chocolate chips, or switch out the vanilla extract for something more exotic.

FOR THE DRY INGREDIENTS:

¾ cup (90 g) whole-wheat pastry flour (*use gluten-free baking mix)

¼ cup (20 g) cocoa powder

¼ cup (60 g) brown sugar

⅛ cup (25 g) sugar

½ teaspoon baking powder

¼ teaspoon salt

FOR THE WET INGREDIENTS:

½ cup (120 ml) unsweetened nondairy milk

2 tablespoons (14 g) ground flaxseeds mixed with ¼ cup (60 ml) warm water

1 teaspoon olive oil (**substitute applesauce or pumpkin purée)

½ teaspoon vanilla extract

Spray the crock with oil or **line with parchment paper to make it oil-free. Mix the dry ingredients in one bowl and the wet ingredients in another. Then add the wet to the dry and mix until combined.

Pour the mixture into the slow cooker and spread evenly on the bottom. Put a clean dish towel or paper towel between the lid and slow cooker to absorb the condensation.

Cook on high for 45 to 90 minutes until the middle is solid and doesn't indent when you touch it.

YIELD: 4 servings
PER SERVING: 210.4 calories; 3.3 g total fat; 1.0 g saturated fat; 3.9 g protein; 43.5 g carbohydrate; 4.1 g dietary fiber; 0 mg cholesterol
PREP TIME: 15 minutes
COOKING TIME: 45 to 90 minutes

RECIPE VARIATION

This recipe really lives in between a brownie and a cake, so I guess you'd call it a cakey brownie. My tester, Ruth, says she added walnuts, which made it even better, so go ahead and add about ¼ cup (30 g) of chopped walnuts if you like. Ruth is always spot-on with her recommendations!

CARROT CAKE RICE PUDDING

★ SOY-FREE   ★ GLUTEN-FREE   ★ OIL-FREE

This rice pudding is great hot or cold, so it works all year long. You can't go wrong with a dessert full of carrots, raisins, nuts, and tons of interesting spices. It may not be as pretty as a cupcake, but it is a pudding after all.

1¼ cups (295 ml) unsweetened nondairy milk

¼ cup (46 g) long-grain brown rice

¼ cup (28 g) grated carrot

⅛ cup (15 g) dried cranberries, blueberries, or (18 g) raisins

⅛ cup (14 g) pecans or (15 g) walnuts, minced

2 tablespoons (10 g) shredded coconut

½ teaspoon vanilla extract

¼ teaspoon ground cinnamon

⅛ teaspoon ground ginger

Pinch cloves

¼ teaspoon stevia plus 1 teaspoon agave nectar or sweetener of your choice, to taste

Add all of the ingredients except for the stevia and agave nectar to your slow cooker. Cook on high for 1½ to 2 hours or until the rice is soft and ready to eat. Mix in the sweetener. You can serve it hot or store in the fridge and eat it chilled.

YIELD: about 2½ cups (640 g)

PER 1-CUP (256 G) SERVING: 177.1 calories; 7.8 g total fat; 2.3 g saturated fat; 3.3 g protein; 23.7 g carbohydrate; 2.6 g dietary fiber; 0.1 mg cholesterol

PREP TIME: 15 minutes

COOKING TIME: 1 ½ to 2 hours

RECIPE VARIATION

Add some vegan cream cheese topping to make this even more decadent. Mix ¼ cup (60 g) vegan cream cheese with 1 teaspoon of lemon juice, 1 teaspoon lemon zest, and just enough agave or stevia to sweeten it a little. Put a dollop on top of each serving.

COCONUT HOT CHOCOLATE

★ SOY-FREE   ★ GLUTEN-FREE

This hot chocolate is not the way to end every night. It's not the healthy redo that many of these recipes are. However, it is a luxurious and decadent drink that's worthy of calling dessert. A little goes a long way, so you can heat up any leftovers the next night or even make just half of the recipe.

1 can (13.5 ounces, or 400 ml) full-fat coconut milk

½ cup (120 ml) unsweetened nondairy milk

½ cup (120 ml) coconut cream

1½ ounces (43 g) vegan semisweet chocolate, chopped

¼ cup (50 g) sugar

Add all the ingredients to your slow cooker and cook on high for 1½ to 2 hours or until it's piping hot and beginning to thicken. Stir once to redistribute the melted chocolate after about 1 hour. This can serve up to 4 in small mugs or 2 in large mugs.

YIELD: about 2½ cups (570 ml)
PER 1-CUP (235 ML) SERVING: 372.2 calories; 26.7 g total fat; 7.1 g saturated fat; 1.3 g protein; 35.0 g carbohydrate; 2.2 g dietary fiber; 0 mg cholesterol
PREP TIME: 10 minutes
COOKING TIME: 1½ to 2 hours

RECIPE VARIATIONS

- If you can't find canned coconut cream in your area, just refrigerate a can of full-fat coconut milk for a few hours and scoop the fat off the top and whip it up. You can use the leftover liquid in place of water or nondairy milk in oatmeal or baked goods. You can health it up a bit by leaving out the coconut cream and using unsweetened chocolate and your choice of sweetener to taste. It will not be as thick, though.

- Make it an adult evening treat by adding a little amaretto or Kahlua.

LAVENDER ROSE VALENTINE COCOA

★ SOY-FREE ★ GLUTEN-FREE ★ OIL-FREE

This is a cocoa that breaks the hot chocolate mold. There's just enough lavender and rosewater to bring a unique, but not overpowering, flavor to this drink. Serve it for Valentine's Day on a saucer sprinkled with fresh or dried rose petals and bits of dried lavender. Your sweetie will love it!

3 cups (700 ml) unsweetened So Delicious Coconut Milk or other nondairy milk

⅓ cup (67 g) sugar

2 ounces (55 g) semisweet vegan baking chocolate, in disks or chopped

¼ teaspoon lavender extract

¼ teaspoon rosewater

Add all the ingredients and cook on low for 2 to 3 hours or on high for 1 to 1½ hours.

Stir once or twice during this time with a whisk to help the chocolate mix in well. Whisk a final time and serve.

YIELD: 3½ cups (820 ml)
PER 1-CUP (235 ML) SERVING: 195.8 calories; 9.4 g total fat; 7.1 g saturated fat; 1.5 g protein; 28.9 g carbohydrate; 1.1 g dietary fiber; 0 mg cholesterol
PREP TIME: 15 minutes
COOKING TIME: 2 to 3 hours on low or 1 to 1½ hours on high

RECIPE VARIATIONS
- I love floral flavors, especially in chocolate, but if you aren't a fan, substitute ½ teaspoon vanilla or orange extract for the rosewater and lavender extract.
- I get my lavender extract at Raleigh's Savory Spice Shop in North Carolina, but you can also get it at savoryspiceshop.com.

SPICE RESOURCES

I've tried to keep most of the recipes pretty basic, but there may be a few spices in these recipes that you aren't familiar with yet. If you have a nearby co-op or place that sells bulk spices, then that should be your first stop. You can get amounts smaller than a teaspoon so you aren't investing a fortune in something you might not even like.

Indian groceries are a perfect and inexpensive source for spices. Hispanic groceries are a playground of fresh and dried chiles. You can toast the whole dried chiles in the oven until crumbly, but not burnt, and grind them in a spice grinder for the freshest chili powder you will ever taste!

My Spice Sage (www.myspicesage.com) is the online spice shop that I use the most. I met the owner at a conference, and we instantly connected. They have tons of exotic blends and are a great source for Indian spices and blends.

They have a huge selection and free shipping in the United States with a minimum purchase. When you buy a little more, you receive whatever premium spice they are featuring for free, and a free 1-ounce (28 g) spice pick of your choice from a huge list with every order. I've gotten saffron and vanilla beans as premiums along with spice blends for particular Indian dishes, free samples of things I wanted to try. You can see why it's become my favorite and why my spices are overflowing everywhere!

Here are other online spice sources to explore:

Savory Spice Shop (www.savoryspiceshop.com) is a small chain, but they also have an online store if there's not one in your area. Their extracts are amazing!

Penzeys (www.penzeys.com) is another chain that's chock-full of choices. They have a catalog and an online store.

Frontier (www.frontiercoop.com/ourproducts.php) is the brand you'll usually find in bulk bins locally, but you can also order online.

ABOUT THE AUTHOR

Kathy Hester, author of *The Great Vegan Bean Book* and the best-selling *The Vegan Slow Cooker*, enjoys spreading the word about how easy it is to make tasty vegan food.

She writes healthyslowcooking.com, is the vegan blogger for Key Ingredient (www.keyingredient.com/blog/bloggers/kathy-hester), and writes for various publications, including *Chickpea Magazine*. She also teaches vegan cooking classes, has put together social media classes for writers, and has more classes in the works.

Just in case you were wondering, Kathy has even more slow cookers now that she's completed another slow cooker book, but she's trying really hard not to buy anymore. She resides in Durham, North Carolina, with a grown-up picky eater in a quirky 1970s modernist house. Her new house is big enough for the cats and the dog to finally all get along, and now they all hang out on the deck together while she cooks and writes.

ACKNOWLEDGMENTS

Amanda Waddell was a huge support and helped me shape this book into what it is. I am always grateful to Lisa and Sally Ekus for representing me and how wonderful they are to work with.

The wonderful photography is the work of photographer Kate Lewis, www.kk-lewis.com.

My fearless testers are amazing people and cooks, plus they made this a better book: Rochelle Arvizo, Monika Soria Caruso, Kimber Cherry, Julie Cross, Jamie Coble, Faith Hood, Mary Harris, Ruth Zagg, and Stephanie Stanesby.

A salute to all my friends who hung in there with me all year while I spent almost all my free time writing cookbooks.

Thanks to Cara Connors and Karen Levy for doing a great editing job. I am so thrilled with Duckie Designs' beautiful layout for this book, under Heather's expert guidance. It was my pleasure to work with Betsy Gammons again—she's a great project manager.

I can't possibly thank Cheryl Purser enough, but she did get a big flat-screen TV and a trip to Disney so that should ease the pain a little bit!

RECIPE LIST

INDEX